chicken
essentials

exciting new ways with a classic ingredient

linda fraser

HERMES
HOUSE

This edition published by Hermes House in 2002

© Anness Publishing Limited 1998, 2002

Hermes House is an imprint of Anness Publishing Limited
Hermes House, 88–89 Blackfriars Road, London SE1 8HA

A CIP catalogue record for this book is available from the British Library.

Publisher: Joanna Lorenz
Cookery Editors: Rosemary Wilkinson, Linda Doeser
Designers: Bill Mason, Siân Keogh
Illustrator: Anna Koska

Recipes: Catherine Atkinson, Alex Barker, Ruby Le Bois, Carla Capalbo, Maxine Clark, Andi Clevely,
Christine France, Carole Handslip, Sarah Gates, Shirley Gill, Norma MacMillan, Sue Maggs, Katherine
Richmond, Jenny Stacey, Liz Trigg, Hilaire Walden, Laura Washburn, Steven Wheeler
Photographers: Karl Adamson, Edward Allwright, Steve Baxter, James Duncan, John Freeman,
Michelle Garrett, Amanda Heywood, Don Last
Food for Photography: Marilyn Forbes, Carole Handslip, Jane Harsthorn, Cara Hobday, Beverly LeBlanc,
Wendy Lee, Lucy McKelvie, Jenny Shapter, Elizabeth Silver, Jane Stevenson,
Liz Trigg, Elizabeth Wolf-Cohen

1 3 5 7 9 10 8 6 4 2

Front cover shows Chicken Breasts Cooked in Butter, for recipe see page 28

Previously published as *Essential Chicken*

NOTES
For all recipes, quantities are given in both metric and imperial measures and, where appropriate,
measures are given in standard cups and spoons. Follow one set, but not a mixture, because they
are not interchangeable.

Standard spoon and cup measurements are level.
1 tsp = 5ml, 1 tbsp = 15ml; 1 cup = 250ml/8fl oz

Australian standard tablespoons are 20ml. Australian readers should use 3 tsp in place of 1 tbsp
for measuring small quantities of gelatine, cornflour, salt etc.

Medium eggs should be used unless otherwise stated.

CONTENTS

Introduction

Chicken is one of the most astonishingly versatile ingredients in any kitchen, anywhere in the world. Delicious, nutritious, economical and with a distinctive flavour of its own, it combines superbly with all kinds of other ingredients – from herbs and spices to vegetables and pasta, and from cream and yogurt to soy and chilli sauces. You can roast, casserole or pot roast the whole bird or cook separate portions, from drumsticks and wings, to boned breasts and other jointed cuts, as well as preparing made-in-minutes dishes from sliced, chopped or minced breast and thigh.

This book is crammed with mouth-watering ways of preparing chicken, some familiar and others rather more unusual. It is divided into six chapters. Soups & Starters offers a collection of warming, filling broths, as well as lighter first courses. Meals in Minutes includes delicious quick and easy recipes to provide interesting, filling and tasty meals for the family throughout the year. Casseroles and Bakes offers a choice of traditional "winter warmers", while Salads, Barbecues & Grills is packed full of recipes just right for warm summer evenings. Roasts & Pies offers both traditional and new ways with chicken, while Hot & Spicy provides a fiery finale!

A useful introductory section offers guidance on choosing whole birds and individual cuts of chicken, step-by-step instructions on trussing, advice on roasting, a selection of scrumptious stuffings and hints on making that invaluable stand-by, chicken stock.

Chicken is easy to prepare and cook, whether fresh or frozen, whole or jointed. Make sure that frozen chicken, especially when still on the bone, is completely thawed before you start to prepare it and that all chicken is thoroughly cooked before you serve it.

chicken
essentials

Choosing a Chicken

A fresh chicken should have a plump breast and the skin should be creamy in colour. The tip of the breast bone should be pliable.

A bird's dressed weight is taken after plucking and drawing and may include the giblets (neck, gizzard, heart and liver). A frozen chicken must be thawed slowly in the fridge or a cool room. Never put it in hot water, as this will toughen the flesh and is dangerous as it allows bacteria to multiply.

Poussins
These are four to six weeks old and weigh 450g–550g/1–1¹/₄lb. One is enough for one person.

Double poussins
These are eight to ten weeks old and weigh 800–900g/1³/₄–2lb. One will serve two people. Poussins are best roasted, grilled or pot-roasted.

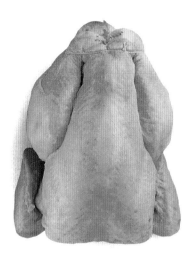

Roasters
These birds are about six to twelve months old and weigh 1.5–2kg/3–4lb. One will feed a family.

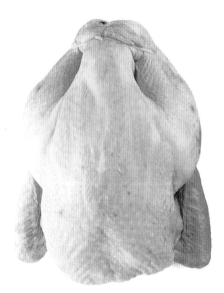

Boilers
These are about twelve months and over and weigh between 2–3kg/4–6lb. They require long, slow cooking, around 2–3 hours, to make them tender.

Corn-fed chickens
These are free-range birds, and are generally more expensive. They usually weigh 1.25–1.5kg/2¹/₂–3lb.

Spring chickens
These birds are about three months old and weigh 900g–1.25kg/2–2¹/₂lb. One will serve three to four people.

Cuts of Chicken

Chicken pieces are available pre-packaged in various forms. If you do not want to buy a whole bird, you can make your choice from the many selected cuts on the market.

Some cooking methods are especially suited to specific cuts of poultry.

Liver

This makes a wonderful addition to pâtés or to salads.

Drumstick

The drumstick is a firm favourite for barbecuing or frying, either in batter or rolled in breadcrumbs.

Wing

The wing does not supply much meat, and is often barbecued or fried.

Thigh

The thigh is suitable for casseroling and other slow-cooking methods.

Skinless boneless thigh

This makes tasks such as stuffing and rolling much quicker, as it is already skinned and jointed.

Breast

The tender white meat can be simply cooked in butter, or can be stuffed for extra flavour.

Minced chicken

This is not as strongly flavoured as, say, ground beef but it may be used as a substitute in some recipes.

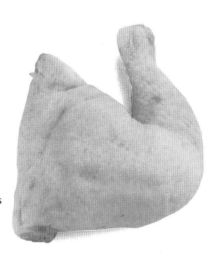

Leg

This comprises the drumstick and thigh. Large pieces with bones, such as this, are suitable for slow-cooking, such as casseroling or poaching.

Trussing Poultry

Trussing holds a bird together during cooking so that it keeps a neat, attractive shape. If the bird is stuffed, trussing prevents the stuffing falling out. You can truss with strong string or with poultry skewers.

An alternative to the method shown here is to use a long trussing needle and fine cotton string: make two passes, in alternate directions, through the body at the open end, from wing to wing, and tie. Then pass the needle through the parson's nose and tie the string around the ends of the drumsticks.

Remove trussing before serving.

1 For an unstuffed bird: set it breast down and pull the neck skin over the neck opening. Turn the bird breast up and fold each wing tip back, over the skin, to secure firmly behind the shoulder.

2 Press the legs firmly down and into the breast. If there is a band of skin across the parson's nose, fold back the ends of the drumsticks and tuck them under the skin.

3 Otherwise, cross the knuckle ends of the drumsticks or bring them tightly together. Loop a length of string several times around the drumstick ends, tie a knot and trim off excess string.

4 For a stuffed bird: fold the wing tips back as above. After stuffing the neck end, fold the flap of skin over the opening and secure it with a skewer, then fold over the wing tips.

5 Put any stuffing or flavourings (herbs, lemon halves, apple quarters and so on) in the body cavity, then secure the ends of the drumsticks as above, tying in the parson's nose, too.

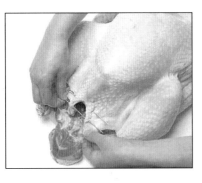

6 Or, the cavity opening can be closed with skewers: insert two or more skewers across the opening, threading them through the skin several times.

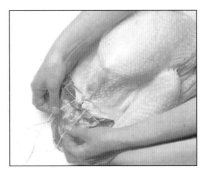

7 Lace the skewers together with string. Tie the drumsticks together over the skewers.

STUFFING TIPS

Only use stuffing that is cool, not hot or chilled. Pack it loosely in the bird and cook any leftovers separately. Stuff poultry just before cooking. Do not stuff the body cavity of a large bird because this could inhibit heat penetration, and thus harmful bacteria may not be destroyed.

Roasting Poultry

Where would family gatherings be without the time-honoured roast bird? But beyond the favourite chicken, all types of poultry can be roasted – from small poussins to large turkeys. However, older tougher birds are better pot-roasted.

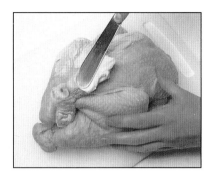

1 Wipe the bird inside and out with damp kitchen paper, stuff, if directed, and truss it. Spread the breast of chicken with soft butter or oil; bard a lean game bird; prick the skin of duck or goose.

2 Set the bird breast up on a rack in a small roasting tin or shallow baking dish. If you are roasting a lean game bird, set the bird in the tin breast down.

3 Roast the bird, basting every 10 minutes after the first 30 minutes with the juices and fat in the tin. Turn if directed. If browning too quickly, cover with foil.

4 Put the bird on a carving board and leave to rest for at least 15 minutes before serving. Meanwhile make a simple sauce or gravy with the juices in the tin.

SIMPLE ROAST CHICKEN

Squeeze the juice from a halved lemon over a 1.35–1.5kg/3–3^1/2lb chicken, then push the lemon halves into the body cavity. Smear 15g/^{1}/2oz softened butter over the breast. Roast in a 190°C/375°F/Gas 5 oven for about 1^1/4 hours. Skim all fat from the roasting juices, then add 120ml/4fl oz/^{1}/2 cup water and bring to the boil, stirring well to mix in the browned bits. Season with salt and pepper, and serve this sauce with the chicken. Serves 4.

ROASTING TIMES FOR POULTRY

Note: Cooking times given here are for unstuffed birds.
For stuffed birds, add 20 minutes to the total roasting time.

POUSSIN	450–700g/1–1^1/2lb	1–1^1/4 hours at 180°C/350°F/Gas 4
CHICKEN	1.12–1.35kg/2^1/2–3lb	1–1^1/4 hours at 190°C/375°F/Gas 5
	1.5–1.8kg/3^1/2–4lb	1^1/4–2 hours at 190°C/375°F/Gas 5
	2.2–2.25kg/4^1/2–5lb	1^1/2–2 hours at 190°C/375°F/Gas 5
	2.25–2.7kg/5–6lb	1^3/4–2^1/2 hours at 190°C/375°F/Gas 5
DUCK	1.35–2.25kg/3–5lb	1^3/4–2^1/4 hours at 200°C/400°F/Gas 6
GOOSE	3.6–4.5kg/8–10lb	2^1/2–3 hours at 180°C/350°F/Gas 4
	4.5–5.4kg/10–12lb	3–3^1/2 hours at 180°C/350°F/Gas 4
TURKEY (whole bird)	2.7–3.6kg/6–8lb	3–3^1/2 hours at 160°C/325°F/Gas 3
	3.6–5.4kg/8–12lb	3–4 hours at 160°C/325°F/Gas 3
	5.4–7.2kg/12–16lb	4–5 hours at 160°C/325°F/Gas 3
TURKEY (whole breast)	1.8–2.7kg/4–6lb	1^1/2–2^1/4 hours at 160°C/325°F/Gas 3
	2.7–3.6kg/6–8lb	2^1/4–3^1/4 hours at 160°C/325°F/Gas 3

PROTECT & FLAVOUR

Before roasting, loosen the skin on the breast by gently easing it away from the flesh with your fingers. Press in softened butter – mixed with herbs or garlic for extra flavour – and smooth back the skin. To bard poultry, cover the breast with slices of bacon before roasting.

Five Stuffings for Chicken

BASIC HERB STUFFING

INGREDIENTS

1 small onion, finely chopped

15g/^{1}/2oz/1 tbsp butter

115g/4oz/2 cups fresh breadcrumbs

15ml/1 tbsp chopped fresh parsley

5ml/1 tsp mixed dried herbs

1 egg, beaten

salt and black pepper

Cook the onion gently in the butter until tender. Allow to cool.

Add to the remaining ingredients and then mix thoroughly. Season well with salt and pepper.

VARIATIONS

Any of these ingredients may be added to the basic recipe to vary the flavour of the stuffing, depending on what you have in your store cupboard at home.

1 celery stick, finely chopped

1 small eating apple, diced

50g/2oz/^{1}/2 cup chopped walnuts or almonds

25g/1oz/1 tbsp raisins or sultanas

50g/2oz/^{1}/4 cup chopped dried prunes or apricots

50g/2oz mushrooms, finely chopped

grated rind of ^{1}/2 orange or lemon

50g/2oz/^{1}/2 cup pine nuts

2 rashers streaky bacon, chopped

APRICOT AND ORANGE STUFFING

INGREDIENTS

1 small onion, finely chopped

15g/^{1}/2 oz/1 tbsp butter

115g/4oz/2 cups fresh breadcrumbs

50g/2oz/^{1}/4 cup finely chopped dried apricots

grated rind of ^{1}/2 orange

1 small egg, beaten

15ml/1 tbsp chopped fresh parsley

salt and black pepper

Heat the butter in a frying pan and cook the onion gently until tender.

Allow to cool slightly, and add to the rest of the ingredients. Mix until thoroughly combined and season with salt and pepper.

RAISIN AND NUT STUFFING

INGREDIENTS

115g/4oz/2 cups fresh breadcrumbs

50g/2oz/^{1}/3 cup raisins

50g/2oz/^{1}/2 cup walnuts, almonds, pistachios or pine nuts

15ml/1 tbsp chopped fresh parsley

5ml/1 tsp chopped mixed herbs

1 small egg, beaten

25g/1oz/2 tbsp melted butter

salt and black pepper

Mix all the ingredients together thoroughly. Season well with salt and pepper.

Raisin and Nut Stuffing

PARSLEY, LEMON AND THYME STUFFING

INGREDIENTS

115g/4oz/2 cups fresh breadcrumbs

25g/1oz/2 tbsp butter

15ml/1 tbsp chopped fresh parsley

2.5ml/^{1}/2 tsp dried thyme

grated rind of ^{1}/4 lemon

1 rasher streaky bacon, chopped

1 small egg, beaten

salt and black pepper

Mix all the ingredients together to combine them thoroughly.

Parsley, Lemon and Thyme Stuffing

SAUSAGEMEAT STUFFING

INGREDIENTS

15g/^{1}/2 oz/1 tbsp butter

1 small onion, finely chopped

2 rashers streaky bacon, chopped

225g/8oz sausagemeat

2.5ml/^{1}/2 tsp mixed dried herbs

salt and black pepper

Heat the butter in a frying pan and cook the onion until tender. Add the bacon and cook for 5 minutes, then allow to cool.

Add to the remaining ingredients and mix thoroughly.

Making Poultry Stock

A good home-made poultry stock is invaluable in the kitchen. It is simple and economical to make, and can be stored in the freezer for up to 6 months. If poultry giblets are available, add them (except the livers) with the wings.

INGREDIENTS

Makes about 2.5 litres/4 pints/10 cups

1.12–1.35kg/2^1/$_2$–3lb poultry wings, backs and necks (chicken, turkey, etc)

2 onions, unpeeled, quartered

4 litres/7 pints cold water

2 carrots, roughly chopped

2 celery stalks, with leaves if possible, roughly chopped

a small handful of fresh parsley

a few fresh thyme sprigs or ^{3}/$_4$ tsp dried thyme

1 or 2 bay leaves

10 black peppercorns, lightly crushed

FRUGAL STOCK

Stock can be made from the bones and carcasses of roasted poultry, cooked with vegetables and flavourings. Save the carcasses in a plastic bag in the freezer until you have three or four, then make stock. It may not have quite as rich a flavour as stock made from a whole bird or fresh wings, backs and necks, but it will still taste fresher and less salty than stock made from a commercial cube.

1 Combine the poultry wings, backs and necks and the onions in a stockpot. Cook over moderate heat until the poultry and onion pieces are lightly browned, stirring from time to time so they colour evenly.

3 Add the remaining ingredients. Partially cover the stockpot and gently simmer the stock for about 3 hours.

5 When cold, carefully remove the layer of fat that will have set on the surface.

2 Add the water and stir well to mix in the sediment on the bottom of the pot. Bring to the boil and skim off the impurities as they rise to the surface of the stock.

4 Strain the stock into a bowl and leave to cool, then refrigerate.

STOCK TIPS

If wished, use a whole bird for making stock instead of wings, backs and necks. A boiling fowl, if available, will give wonderful flavour and provide meat to use in salads, sandwiches, soups and casseroles.

No salt is added to stock because as the stock reduces, the flavour becomes concentrated and saltiness increases. Add salt to dishes which contain the stock.

SOUPS &
STARTERS

Smoked Chicken and Lentil Soup

Smoked chicken gives added depth of flavour to this hearty soup.

INGREDIENTS

Serves 4

25g/1oz/2 tbsp butter

1 large carrot, chopped

1 onion, chopped

1 celery stick, chopped

1 leek, white part only, chopped

115g/4oz/1^1/$_2$ cups mushrooms, chopped

50ml/2fl oz/^{1}/$_4$ cup dry white wine

1 litre/1^3/$_4$ pints/4 cups chicken stock

10ml/2 tsp dried thyme

1 bay leaf

120ml/4fl oz/^{1}/$_2$ cup lentils

225g/8oz/1^1/$_2$ cups smoked
    chicken meat, diced

salt and pepper

chopped fresh parsley, to garnish

1 Melt the butter in a large saucepan. Add the carrot, onion, celery, leek and mushrooms. Cook gently until golden, about 3–5 minutes.

2 Stir in the wine and chicken stock. Bring to the boil and skim any foam that rises to the surface. Add the thyme and bay leaf. Lower the heat, cover, and simmer gently for 30 minutes.

3 Add the lentils and continue cooking, covered, until they are just tender, 30–40 minutes more. Stir the soup from time to time.

4 Stir in the chicken and season to taste. Cook until just heated through. Ladle into bowls and garnish with chopped parsley.

Mulligatawny Soup

Mulligatawny (which means "pepper water") was introduced into England in the late eighteenth century, by members of the army and colonial service returning home from India.

INGREDIENTS

Serves 4

50g/2oz/4 tbsp butter or 60ml/4 tbsp oil

2 large chicken joints, about
   350g/12oz each

1 onion, chopped

1 carrot, chopped

1 small turnip, chopped

about 15ml/1 tbsp curry powder, to taste

4 cloves

6 black peppercorns, lightly crushed

50g/2oz/$^1/_4$ cup lentils

900ml/1$^1/_2$ pints/3$^3/_4$ cups chicken stock

40g/1$^1/_2$ oz/$^1/_4$ cup sultanas

salt and pepper

1 Melt the butter or heat the oil in a large saucepan and brown the chicken over a brisk heat. Transfer the chicken on to a plate.

COOK'S TIP

Red split lentils will give the best colour for this dish, although green or brown lentils could be used if you prefer.

2 Add the onion, carrot and turnip to the pan and cook, stirring occasionally, until lightly coloured. Stir in the curry powder, cloves and peppercorns and cook for 1–2 minutes. Add the lentils.

3 Pour in the stock and bring to the boil. Add the sultanas and chicken and any juices from the plate. Cover and simmer gently for about 1$^1/_4$ hours.

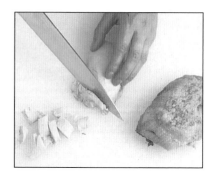

4 Remove the chicken from the pan and discard the skin and bones. Chop the flesh, return to the soup and reheat. Check and adjust the seasoning before serving the soup piping hot.

Chicken Vermicelli Soup with Egg Shreds

This light soup can be put together in a matter of moments and is full of flavour.

INGREDIENTS

Serves 4–6

3 size 1 eggs

30ml/2 tbsp chopped fresh coriander or parsley

1.5 litres/$2^{1}/_{2}$ pints/$6^{1}/_{4}$ cups good chicken stock or canned consommé

115g/4oz/1 cup dried vermicelli or angel hair pasta

115g/4oz cooked chicken breast, sliced

salt and pepper

1 First make the egg shreds. Whisk the eggs together in a small bowl and stir in the chopped coriander or parsley.

2 Heat a small non-stick frying pan and pour in 30–45ml/ 2–3 tbsp egg, swirling to cover the base evenly. Cook until set. Repeat until all the mixture is used up.

3 Roll each pancake up and slice thinly into shreds. Set aside.

4 Bring the stock to the boil and add the pasta, breaking it into short lengths. Cook for 3–5 minutes until the pasta is almost tender, then add the chicken, salt and pepper. Heat through for 2–3 minutes, then stir in the egg shreds. Serve immediately.

Thai Chicken Soup

This filling and tasty soup is very quick to prepare and cook.

INGREDIENTS

Serves 4

15ml/1 tbsp vegetable oil

1 garlic clove, finely chopped

2 boned chicken breasts, about 175g/6oz each, skinned and chopped

2.5ml/$\frac{1}{2}$ tsp ground turmeric

1.5ml/$\frac{1}{4}$ tsp hot chilli powder

75g/3oz creamed coconut

900ml/1$\frac{1}{2}$ pints/3$\frac{3}{4}$ cups hot chicken stock

30ml/2 tbsp lemon or lime juice

30ml/2 tbsp crunchy peanut butter

50g/2oz/1 cup thread egg noodles, broken into small pieces

15ml/1 tbsp spring onions, finely chopped

15ml/1 tbsp chopped fresh coriander

salt and black pepper

30ml/2 tbsp desiccated coconut and $\frac{1}{2}$ fresh red chilli, seeded and finely chopped, to garnish

1 Heat the oil in a large pan and fry the garlic for 1 minute until lightly golden. Add the chicken and spices and stir-fry for a further 3–4 minutes.

2 Crumble the creamed coconut into the hot chicken stock and stir until dissolved. Pour on to the chicken and add the lemon juice, peanut butter and egg noodles.

3 Cover the pan and simmer for about 15 minutes.

4 Add the spring onions and fresh coriander, then season well and cook for a further 5 minutes. Meanwhile, place the desiccated coconut and chilli in a small frying pan and heat for 2–3 minutes, stirring frequently.

5 Serve the soup in bowls and sprinkle each one with some fried coconut and chilli.

Chicken Cigars

These small crispy rolls can be served warm as canapés with a drink before a meal, or as a first course with a crisp, colourful salad.

INGREDIENTS

Serves 4

275g/10oz packet of filo pastry

45ml/3 tbsp olive oil

fresh parsley, to garnish

For the filling

350g/12oz/3 cups minced raw chicken

salt and freshly ground black pepper

1 egg, beaten

2.5ml/^{1}/2 tsp ground cinnamon

2.5ml/^{1}/2 tsp ground ginger

30ml/2 tbsp raisins

15ml/1 tbsp olive oil

1 small onion, finely chopped

1 Mix all the filling ingredients, except the oil and onion, together in a bowl. Heat the oil in a large frying pan and cook the onion until tender. Leave to cool. Add the mixed filling ingredients.

2 Preheat the oven to 180°C/ 350°F/Gas 4. Once the filo pastry packet has been opened, keep the pastry covered at all times with a damp dish towel. Work fast, as the pastry dries out very quickly when exposed to the air. Unravel the pastry and cut into 25 x 10cm/ 10 x 4in strips.

3 Take a strip (cover the remainder), brush with a little oil and place a small spoonful of filling about 1cm/^{1}/2in from the end.

4 To encase the filling, fold the sides inwards to a width of 5cm/2in and roll into a cigar shape. Place on a greased baking sheet and brush with oil. Repeat to use all the filling. Bake for about 20–25 minutes until golden brown and crisp. Garnish with fresh parsley and serve.

Chicken Liver Pâté

*A deliciously smooth pâté which is
ideal to spread on hot toast.*

INGREDIENTS

Serves 6 or more

50g/2oz/4 tbsp butter

1 onion, finely chopped

350g/12oz chicken livers, trimmed of all
   dark or greenish parts

60ml/4 tbsp medium sherry

25g/1oz full-fat soft cheese

15–30ml/1–2 tbsp lemon juice

2 hard-boiled eggs, chopped

salt and pepper

50–75g/2–3oz/¼ cup clarified butter

1 Melt the butter in a frying pan.
Add the onion and livers and
cook until the onion is soft and the
livers are lightly browned and no
longer pink in the centre.

2 Add the sherry and boil until
reduced by half. Cool slightly.

COOK'S TIP
∼

Add brandy instead of sherry for
a special occasion dinner party.

3 Turn the mixture into a food
processor or blender and add
the soft cheese and 1 tablespoon
lemon juice. Blend until smooth.

4 Add the hard-boiled eggs and
blend briefly. Season with salt
and pepper. Taste and add more
lemon juice if liked.

5 Pack the liver pâté into a
mould or into individual
ramekins. Smooth the surface.

6 Spoon a layer of clarified
butter over the surface of the
pâté. Chill until firm. Serve at
room temperature, with hot toast
or savoury biscuits.

Chicken and Avocado Mayonnaise

You need quite firm scoops or forks to eat this starter, so don't be tempted to try to pass it round as a finger food.

INGREDIENTS

Serves 4

30ml/2 tbsp mayonnaise

15ml/1 tbsp fromage frais

2 garlic cloves, crushed

115g/4oz/1 cup chopped cooked chicken

1 large ripe, but firm, avocado,
   peeled and stoned

30ml/2 tbsp lemon juice

salt and black pepper

nacho chips or tortilla chips, to serve

1 Mix together the mayonnaise, fromage frais, garlic, and seasoning to taste, in a small bowl. Stir in the chopped chicken.

COOK'S TIP

This mixture also makes a great, chunky filling for sandwiches, baps or pitta bread. Or serve as a main course salad, heaped on to a base of mixed salad leaves.

2 Chop the avocado and toss immediately in lemon juice.

3 Mix the avocado gently into the chicken mixture. Check the seasoning and chill until required.

4 Serve in small serving dishes with the nacho or tortilla chips as scoops, if liked.

MEALS IN MINUTES

Monday Savoury Omelette

Use up all the leftover odds and ends in this tasty omelette.

INGREDIENTS

Serves 4–6

30ml/2 tbsp olive oil

1 large onion, chopped

2 large garlic cloves, crushed

115g/4oz rindless bacon, chopped

50g/2oz cold cooked chicken, chopped

115g/4oz leftover cooked vegetables
  (preferably ones which are not too soft)

115g/4oz/1 cup leftover cooked
  rice or pasta

4 eggs

30ml/2 tbsp chopped, mixed fresh herbs,
  such as parsley, chives, marjoram or tarragon, or 10ml/2 tsp dried

5ml/1 tsp Worcestershire sauce,
  or more to taste

15ml/1 tbsp grated mature
  Cheddar cheese

salt and black pepper

1 Heat the oil in a large flame-proof frying pan and sauté the onion, garlic and bacon until all the fat has run out of the bacon.

2 Add the chopped meat, vegetables and rice. Beat the eggs, herbs and Worcestershire sauce together with seasoning. Pour over the rice or pasta and vegetables, stir lightly, then leave the mixture undisturbed to cook gently for about 5 minutes.

3 When just beginning to set, sprinkle with the cheese and place under a preheated grill until just firm and golden.

COOK'S TIP

This is surprisingly good cold, so is perfect for taking on picnics, or using for packed lunches.

Tagliatelle with Chicken and Herb Sauce

This wine-flavoured sauce is best served with green salad.

INGREDIENTS

Serves 4

30ml/2 tbsp olive oil

1 red onion, cut into wedges

350g/12oz tagliatelle

1 garlic clove, chopped

350g/12oz/2^1/$_2$ cups chicken, diced

300ml/^{1}/$_2$ pint/1^1/$_4$ cups dry vermouth

45ml/3 tbsp chopped fresh mixed herbs

150ml/^{1}/$_4$ pint/^{2}/$_3$ cup fromage frais

salt and black pepper

shredded fresh mint, to garnish

1 Heat the oil in a large frying pan and fry the onion for 10 minutes until softened and the layers separate.

2 Cook the pasta in plenty of water following the instructions on the packet.

COOK'S TIP

If you don't want to use vermouth, use dry white wine instead. Orvieto and frascati are two Italian wines that are ideal to use in this sauce.

3 Add the garlic and chicken to the pan and fry for 10 minutes, stirring occasionally until the chicken is browned all over and cooked through.

4 Pour in the vermouth, bring to the boil and boil rapidly until reduced by about half.

5 Stir in the herbs, fromage frais and seasoning and heat through gently, but do not boil.

6 Drain the pasta thoroughly and toss it with the sauce to coat. Serve immediately, garnished with shredded fresh mint.

Penne with Chicken and Ham Sauce

A meal in itself, this colourful pasta sauce is perfect for lunch or dinner.

INGREDIENTS

Serves 4

350g/12oz/3 cups penne pasta

25g/1oz/2 tbsp butter

1 onion, chopped

1 garlic clove, chopped

1 bay leaf

475ml/16 fl oz/2 cups dry white wine

150ml/^{1}/$_4$ pint/^{2}/$_3$ cup crème fraîche

225g/8oz/1^1/$_2$ cups cooked chicken,
   skinned, boned and diced

115g/4oz/^{2}/$_3$ cup cooked lean ham, diced

115g/4oz/1 cup Gouda cheese, grated

15ml/1 tbsp chopped fresh mint

salt and black pepper

finely shredded fresh mint, to garnish

1 Cook the pasta in plenty of water following the instructions on the packet.

2 Heat the butter in a large frying pan and fry the onion for 10 minutes until softened.

COOK'S TIP

Crème fraîche is a richer, full-fat French cream with a slightly acidic taste. If you can't find any, substitute soured cream.

3 Add the garlic, bay leaf and wine and bring to the boil. Boil rapidly until reduced by half. Remove the bay leaf, then stir in the crème fraîche and bring back to the boil.

4 Add the chicken, ham and cheese and simmer for 5 minutes, stirring occasionally until heated through.

5 Add the mint and seasoning. Drain the pasta and turn it into a large serving bowl. Toss with the sauce immediately and garnish with shredded mint.

Chicken and Shiitake Mushroom Pizza

The addition of shiitake mushrooms adds an earthy flavour to this colourful pizza, while fresh red chilli gives a hint of spiciness.

INGREDIENTS

Serves 3–4

45ml/3 tbsp olive oil

350g/12oz/3 cups chicken breast fillets, skinned and cut into thin strips

1 bunch spring onions, sliced

1 fresh red chilli, seeded and chopped

1 red pepper, seeded and cut into thin strips

75g/3oz fresh shiitake mushrooms, wiped and sliced

45–60ml/3–4 tbsp chopped fresh coriander

1 pizza base, about 25–30cm/10–12in diameter

15ml/1 tbsp chilli oil

150g/5oz/11/4 cups mozzarella cheese

salt and black pepper

1 Preheat the oven to 220°C/ 425°F/Gas 7. Heat 30ml/2tbsp of the olive oil in a wok or large frying pan. Add the chicken, spring onions, chilli, pepper and mushrooms and stir-fry over a high heat for 2–3 minutes until the chicken is firm but still slightly pink within. Season.

2 Pour off any excess oil, then set aside the chicken mixture until cool.

3 Stir the fresh coriander into the chicken mixture.

4 Brush the pizza base with the chilli oil.

5 Spoon over the chicken mixture and drizzle over the remaining olive oil.

6 Grate the mozzarella and sprinkle over. Bake for 15–20 minutes until crisp and golden. Serve immediately.

Chicken and Avocado Pitta Pizzas

Pitta bread is used here to make quick bases for a tasty pizza.

INGREDIENTS

Serves 4

8 plum tomatoes, quartered

45–60ml/3–4 tbsp olive oil

1 large ripe avocado

8 pitta bread rounds

6–7 slices of cooked chicken, chopped

1 onion, thinly sliced

275g/10oz/2^1/2 cups grated Cheddar cheese

30ml/2 tbsp chopped fresh coriander

salt and pepper

1 Preheat the oven to 230°C/450°F/Gas 8.

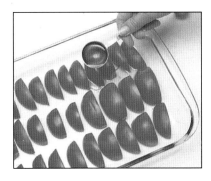

2 Place the tomatoes in a baking dish. Drizzle over 15ml/1 tbsp of the oil and season to taste. Bake for 30 minutes; do not stir.

3 Remove the baking dish from the oven and mash the tomatoes with a fork, removing the skins as you mash. Set aside.

4 Peel and stone the avocado. Cut into 16 thin slices.

5 Brush the edges of the pitta breads with oil. Arrange the breads on two baking sheets.

6 Spread each pitta with mashed tomato, almost to the edges.

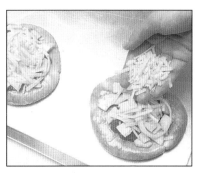

7 Top each with 2 avocado slices. Sprinkle with the chicken, then add a few onion slices. Season to taste. Sprinkle on the cheese.

8 Place one sheet in the middle of the oven and bake until the cheese begins to melt, about 15–20 minutes. Sprinkle with half the coriander and serve. Meanwhile, bake the second batch of pizzas, cook and serve them hot.

Chicken with Peppers

This colourful dish comes from the south of Italy, where sweet peppers are plentiful.

Serves 4

1.5kg/3lb chicken, cut into serving pieces

3 large peppers, red, yellow or green

90ml/6 tbsp olive oil

2 medium red onions, finely sliced

2 cloves garlic, finely chopped

small piece of dried chilli, crumbled (optional)

100ml/4fl oz/^{1}/$_2$ cup white wine

salt and black pepper

2 tomatoes, fresh or canned, peeled and chopped

45g/3 tbsp chopped fresh parsley

1 Trim any fat off the chicken, and remove all excess skin. Prepare peppers by cutting them in half, discarding the seeds and the stem. Slice into strips.

2 Heat half the oil in a large heavy saucepan or casserole. Add the onion, and cook over low heat until soft. Remove to a side dish. Add the remaining oil to the pan, raise the heat to moderate, add the chicken and brown on all sides, 6–8 minutes. Return the onions to the pan, and add the garlic and dried chilli, if using.

3 Pour in the wine, and cook until it has reduced by half. Add the peppers and stir well to coat them with the fats. Season. After 3–4 minutes, stir in the tomatoes. Lower the heat, cover the pan, and cook until the peppers are soft, and the chicken is cooked, about 25–30 minutes. Stir occasionally. Stir in the chopped parsley and serve.

Chicken Breasts Cooked in Butter

This simple and very delicious way of cooking chicken brings out all of its delicacy.

Serves 4

4 small chicken breasts, skinned and boned

flour seasoned with salt and freshly ground black pepper, for dredging

75g/3oz/6 tbsp butter

1 sprig fresh parsley, to garnish

1 Separate the two fillets of each breast. They come apart very easily; one is large, the other small. Pound the large fillets between two sheets of clear film lightly to flatten them. Dredge the chicken in the seasoned flour, shaking off any excess.

2 Heat the butter in a large heavy frying pan until it bubbles. Place all the chicken fillets in the pan, in one layer if possible. Cook over moderate to high heat for 3–4 minutes until they are golden brown.

3 Turn the chicken over. Reduce the heat to low to moderate, and continue cooking until the fillets are cooked through but still springy to the touch, about 9–12 minutes in all. If the chicken begins to brown too much, cover the pan for the final minutes of cooking. Serve at once garnished with a little parsley.

Chicken with Spiced Rice

This is a good dish for entertaining. It can be prepared in advance and reheated in the oven. Serve with traditional curry accompaniments.

INGREDIENTS

Serves 8

900g/2lb boneless chicken thighs

60ml/4 tbsp olive oil

2 large onions, thinly sliced

1–2 green chillies, seeded and finely chopped

5ml/1 tsp grated fresh root ginger

1 garlic clove, crushed

15ml/1 tbsp hot curry powder

150ml/^{1}/4 pint/^{2}/3 cup chicken stock

150ml/^{1}/4 pint/^{2}/3 cup natural yogurt

30ml/2 tbsp chopped fresh coriander

salt and black pepper

For the spiced rice

450g/1lb/generous 2^1/4 cups basmati rice

2.5ml/^{1}/2 tsp garam masala

900ml/1^1/2 pints/3^3/4 cups chicken stock or water

50g/2oz/scant ^{1}/2 cup raisins or sultanas

25g/1oz/^{1}/2 cup toasted chopped almonds

1 Put the basmati rice into a sieve and wash under cold running water to remove any starchy powder coating the grains. Then put into a bowl and cover with cold water and leave to soak for 30 minutes. The grains will absorb some water so that they will not stick together in a solid mass while cooking.

2 Preheat the oven to 160°C/ 325°F/Gas 3. Cut the chicken into cubes of approximately 2.5cm/1in. Heat 30ml/2 tbsp of the oil in a large flameproof casserole, add one onion and cook until softened. Add the finely chopped chillies, ginger, garlic and curry powder and continue cooking for a further 2 minutes, stirring from time to time.

3 Add the stock and seasoning, bring slowly to the boil. Add the chicken. Cover and cook in the oven for 20 minutes or until tender.

4 Remove from the oven and stir in the yogurt.

5 Meanwhile, heat the remaining oil in a flameproof casserole and cook the remaining onion gently until tender and lightly browned. Add the drained rice, garam masala and stock or water. Bring to the boil, cover and cook in the oven with the chicken for 20–35 minutes or until tender and all the stock has been absorbed.

6 To serve, stir the raisins or sultanas and toasted almonds into the rice. Spoon half the rice into a large deep serving dish, cover with the chicken and then the remaining rice. Sprinkle with chopped coriander to garnish.

Chicken Biryani

A deceptively easy curry to make, and very tasty, too.

INGREDIENTS

Serves 4

275g/10oz/1^{1}/$_{2}$ cups basmati rice, rinsed

2.5ml/^{1}/$_{2}$ tsp salt

5 whole cardamom pods

2–3 whole cloves

1 cinnamon stick

45ml/3 tbsp vegetable oil

3 onions, sliced

675g/1^{1}/$_{2}$lb chicken (4 x 175g/6oz chicken breasts), cubed, skinned and boned

1.5ml/^{1}/$_{4}$ tsp ground cloves

5 cardamom pods, seeds removed and ground

1.5ml/^{1}/$_{4}$ tsp hot chilli powder

5ml/1 tsp ground cumin

5ml/1 tsp ground coriander

2.5ml/^{1}/$_{2}$ tsp black pepper

3 garlic cloves, finely chopped

5ml/1 tsp finely chopped fresh root ginger

juice of 1 lemon

4 tomatoes, sliced

30ml/2 tbsp chopped fresh coriander

150ml/^{1}/$_{4}$ pint/^{2}/$_{3}$ cup natural yogurt

2.5ml/^{1}/$_{2}$ tsp saffron strands soaked in 10ml/2 tsp hot milk

45ml/3 tbsp toasted flaked almonds and fresh coriander sprigs, to garnish

natural yogurt, to serve

1 Preheat the oven to 190°C/ 375°F/Gas 5. Bring a pan of water to the boil and add the rice, salt, cardamom pods, cloves and cinnamon stick. Boil for 2 minutes and then drain, leaving the whole spices in the rice.

2 Heat the oil in a pan and fry the onions for 8 minutes, until browned. Add the chicken followed by all the ground spices, the garlic, ginger and lemon juice. Stir-fry for 5 minutes.

3 Transfer the chicken mixture to a casserole and lay the sliced tomatoes on top. Sprinkle over the fresh coriander, spoon over the natural yogurt and top with the drained rice.

4 Drizzle the saffron and milk over the rice and pour over 150ml/^{1}/$_{4}$ pint/^{2}/$_{3}$ cup of water.

5 Cover tightly and bake in the oven for 1 hour. Transfer to a warmed serving platter and remove the whole spices from the rice. Garnish with toasted almonds and fresh coriander and serve with extra natural yogurt.

Chicken Naan Pockets

This quick and easy dish is ideal for a speedy snack, lunch or supper. To save time, use the ready-to-bake naans available in some supermarkets and Asian stores, or try warmed pitta bread instead.

INGREDIENTS

Serves 4

4 ready-prepared naans

45ml/3 tbsp natural low-fat yogurt

7.5ml/1^{1}/2 tsp garam masala

5ml/1 tsp chilli powder

5ml/1 tsp salt

45ml/3 tbsp lemon juice

15ml/1 tbsp chopped fresh coriander

1 green chilli, chopped

450g/1lb/3^{1}/4 cups cubed chicken

15ml/1 tbsp vegetable oil (optional)

8 onion rings

2 tomatoes, quartered

^{1}/2 white cabbage, shredded

To garnish

lemon wedges

2 small tomatoes, halved

mixed salad leaves

fresh coriander

1 Cut into the middle of each naan to make a pocket, then set aside.

2 Mix together the yogurt, garam masala, chilli powder, salt, lemon juice, fresh coriander and chopped green chilli. Pour the marinade over the chicken pieces and leave them to marinate for about 1 hour.

3 Preheat the grill to very hot, then lower the heat to medium. Place the chicken in a flameproof dish and grill for 15–20 minutes until tender and cooked through, turning the chicken at least twice.

4 Remove from the heat and fill each naan with the chicken and then with the onion rings, tomatoes and cabbage. Serve with the garnish ingredients.

Chicken Tikka

This chicken dish is an extremely popular Indian appetizer and is quick and easy to cook. Chicken Tikka can also be served as a main course for four.

INGREDIENTS

Serves 6

450g/1lb/3^{1}/4 cups cubed chicken

5ml/1 tsp chopped fresh root ginger

5ml/1 tsp chopped garlic

5ml/1 tsp chilli powder

1.5ml/^{1}/4 tsp ground turmeric

5ml/1 tsp salt

150ml/^{1}/4 pint/^{2}/3 cup natural low-fat
    yogurt

60ml/4 tbsp lemon juice

15ml/1 tbsp chopped fresh coriander

15ml/1 tbsp vegetable oil

To garnish

1 small onion, cut into rings

lime wedges

mixed salad

fresh coriander

1 In a medium bowl, mix together the chicken pieces, ginger, garlic, chilli powder, turmeric, salt, yogurt, lemon juice and fresh coriander and leave to marinate for at least 2 hours.

2 Place on a grill pan or in a flameproof dish lined with foil and baste with the oil.

3 Preheat the grill to medium. Grill the chicken for 15–20 minutes until cooked, turning and basting two or three times. Serve with the garnish ingredients.

Pan-fried Honey Chicken Drumsticks

The sweetness of the honey contrasts well with the lemon and soy sauce.

INGREDIENTS

Serves 4

115g/4oz/^{1}/$_2$ cup clear honey

juice of 1 lemon

30ml/2 tbsp soy sauce

15ml/1 tbsp sesame seeds

2.5ml/^{1}/$_2$ tsp fresh or dried thyme leaves

12 chicken drumsticks

2.5ml/^{1}/$_2$ tsp salt

2.5ml/^{1}/$_2$ tsp pepper

80g/3^1/$_4$ oz/^{3}/$_4$ cup flour

45ml/3 tbsp butter or margarine

45ml/3 tbsp vegetable oil

120ml/4fl oz/^{1}/$_2$ cup white wine

120ml/4fl oz/^{1}/$_2$ cup chicken stock

1 In a large bowl, combine the honey, lemon juice, soy sauce, sesame seeds and thyme. Add the chicken drumsticks and mix to coat them well. Leave to marinate in a cool place for 2 hours or more, turning occasionally.

2 Mix the salt, pepper and flour in a shallow bowl. Drain the drumsticks, reserving the marinade. Roll them in the seasoned flour to coat all over.

3 Heat the butter or margarine with the oil in a large frying pan. When hot and sizzling, add the drumsticks. Brown them on all sides. Reduce the heat to medium–low and cook until the chicken is done, 12–15 minutes.

4 Test the drumsticks with a fork; the juices should be clear. Remove the drumsticks to a serving platter and keep hot.

5 Pour off most of the fat from the pan. Add the wine, stock and reserved marinade and stir well to mix in the cooking juices on the bottom of the pan. Bring to the boil and simmer until reduced by half. Check and adjust the seasoning, then spoon the sauce over the drumsticks and serve.

Louisiana Rice

A tasty meal of pork, rice, chicken livers and an array of spices.

INGREDIENTS

Serves 4

60ml/4 tbsp vegetable oil

1 small aubergine, diced

225g/8oz minced pork

1 green pepper, seeded and chopped

2 sticks celery, chopped

1 onion, chopped

1 garlic clove, crushed

5ml/1 tsp cayenne pepper

5ml/1 tsp paprika

5ml/1 tsp black pepper

2.5ml/^{1}/$_2$ tsp salt

5ml/1 tsp dried thyme

2.5ml/^{1}/$_2$ tsp dried oregano

475ml/16fl oz/2 cups chicken stock

225g/8oz chicken livers, minced

150g/5oz/^{3}/$_4$ cup long grain rice

1 bay leaf

45ml/3 tbsp chopped fresh parsley

celery leaves, to garnish

1 Heat the oil in a frying pan until really hot, then add the diced aubergine and stir-fry for about 5 minutes.

2 Add the pork and cook for about 6–8 minutes, until browned, using a wooden spoon to break any lumps.

3 Add the chopped green pepper, celery, onion, garlic and all the spices and herbs. Cover and cook on a high heat for 5–6 minutes, stirring frequently from the bottom to scrape up and distribute the crispy brown bits.

4 Pour on the chicken stock and stir to clean the bottom of the pan. Cover and cook for 6 minutes over a moderate heat. Stir in the chicken livers, cook for 2 minutes, then stir in the rice and add the bay leaf.

5 Reduce the heat, cover and simmer for about 6–7 minutes. Turn off the heat and leave to stand for a further 10–15 minutes until the rice is tender. Remove the bay leaf and stir in the chopped parsley. Serve the rice hot, garnished with the celery leaves.

Stir-fried Chicken with Mange-touts

Juicy chicken stir-fried with mange-touts, cashews and water chestnuts.

INGREDIENTS

Serves 4

30ml/2 tbsp sesame oil
90ml/6 tbsp lemon juice
1 garlic clove, crushed
1cm/^{1}/2 in piece fresh root ginger,
   peeled and grated
5ml/1 tsp clear honey
450g/1lb chicken breast fillets,
   cut into strips
115g/4oz mange-touts, trimmed
30ml/2 tbsp groundnut oil
50g/2oz/^{1}/2 cup cashew nuts
6 spring onions, cut into strips
225g/8oz can water chestnuts,
   drained and thinly sliced
salt
saffron rice, to serve

1 Mix together the sesame oil, lemon juice, garlic, ginger and honey in a shallow non-metallic dish. Add the chicken and mix well. Cover and leave to marinate for at least 3–4 hours.

2 Blanch the mange-touts in boiling salted water for 1 minute. Drain and refresh under cold running water.

3 Drain the chicken strips and reserve the marinade. Heat the groundnut oil in a wok or large frying pan, add the cashew nuts and stir-fry for about 1–2 minutes until golden brown. Remove the cashew nuts from the wok or frying pan using a slotted spoon and set aside.

4 Add the chicken and stir-fry for 3–4 minutes, until golden brown. Add the spring onions, mange-touts, water chestnuts and the reserved marinade. Cook for a few minutes, until the chicken is tender and the sauce is bubbling and hot. Stir in the cashew nuts and serve with saffron rice.

Risotto

An Italian dish made with short grain arborio rice which gives a creamy consistency to this easy one-pan recipe.

INGREDIENTS

Serves 4

15ml/1 tbsp oil

175g/6oz/1 cup Arborio rice

1 onion, chopped

225g/8oz/2 cups minced chicken

600ml/1 pint/2$^{1}/_{2}$ cups chicken stock

1 red pepper, seeded and chopped

1 yellow pepper, seeded and
chopped

75g/3oz/$^{3}/_{4}$ cup frozen green beans

115g/4oz/1$^{1}/_{2}$ cups chestnut
mushrooms, sliced

15ml/1 tbsp chopped fresh parsley

salt and black pepper

fresh parsley, to garnish

3 Pour in the stock and bring to
the boil.

4 Stir in the peppers and reduce
the heat. Cook for 10 minutes.

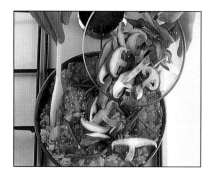

5 Add the green beans and
mushrooms and cook for a
further 10 minutes.

6 Stir in the fresh parsley and
season well to taste. Cook for
10 minutes or until the liquid has
been absorbed. Serve garnished
with fresh parsley.

1 Heat the oil in a large frying
pan. Add the rice and cook for
2 minutes until transparent.

2 Add the onion and minced
chicken. Cook for 5 minutes,
stirring occasionally.

Chicken in Green Sauce

*Slow, gentle cooking makes the
chicken succulent and tender.*

INGREDIENTS

Serves 4

25g/1oz/2 tbsp butter

15ml/1 tbsp olive oil

4 chicken portions

1 small onion, finely chopped

150ml/$^{1}/_{4}$ pint/$^{2}/_{3}$ cup medium dry
   white wine

150ml/$^{1}/_{4}$ pint/$^{2}/_{3}$ cup chicken stock

175g/6oz watercress

2 thyme sprigs and 2 tarragon sprigs

150ml/$^{1}/_{4}$ pint/$^{2}/_{3}$ cup double cream

salt and black pepper

watercress leaves, to garnish

1 Heat the butter and oil in a
heavy shallow pan, then brown
the chicken evenly. Transfer the
chicken to a plate using a slotted
spoon and keep warm in the oven.

2 Add the onion to the cooking
juices in the pan and cook until
softened but not coloured.

3 Stir in the wine, boil for 2–3
minutes, then add the stock
and bring to the boil. Return the
chicken to the pan, cover tightly
and cook very gently for about 30
minutes, until the chicken juices
run clear. Then transfer the
chicken to a warm dish, cover the
dish and keep warm.

4 Boil the cooking juices hard
until reduced to about 60ml/
4 tbsp. Remove the leaves from the
watercress and herbs, add to the
pan with the cream and simmer
over a medium heat until the sauce
has thickened slightly.

5 Return the cooked chicken to
the casserole, season and heat
through for a few minutes.
Garnish with watercress leaves
before serving.

Chicken Stroganov

Based on the classic Russian dish, usually made with fillet of beef. Serve with rice mixed with chopped celery and spring onions.

INGREDIENTS

Serves 4

4 large chicken breasts, boned and
   skinned
45ml/3 tbsp olive oil
1 large onion, thinly sliced
225g/8oz/3 cups mushrooms, sliced
300ml/^{1}/2 pint/1^1/4 cups soured cream
salt and black pepper
15ml/1 tbsp chopped fresh parsley,
   to garnish

1 Divide the chicken breasts into two natural fillets, place between two sheets of clear film and flatten each to a thickness of 1cm/^{1}/2in with a rolling pin.

2 Cut into 2.5cm/1in strips diagonally across the fillets.

3 Heat 30ml/2 tbsp of the oil in a frying pan and cook the onion slowly until soft but not coloured.

4 Add the mushrooms and cook until golden brown. Remove and keep warm.

5 Increase the heat, add the remaining oil and fry the chicken very quickly, in small batches, for 3–4 minutes until lightly coloured. Remove to a dish and keep warm.

6 Return all the chicken, onions and mushrooms to the pan and season with salt and black pepper. Stir in the soured cream and bring to the boil. Sprinkle with fresh parsley and serve immediately.

CASSEROLES
& BAKES

Cannelloni al Forno

A lighter alternative to the usual beef-filled, béchamel-coated version. Fill with ricotta, onion and mushroom for a vegetarian recipe.

INGREDIENTS

Serves 4–6

450g/1lb/4 cups skinned and boned
   chicken breast, cooked
225g/8oz mushrooms
2 garlic cloves, crushed
30ml/2 tbsp chopped fresh parsley
15ml/1 tbsp chopped fresh tarragon
1 egg, beaten
fresh lemon juice
12–18 cannelloni tubes
475ml/16 fl oz/2 cups ready-made tomato
   sauce
50g/2oz/²⁄₃ cup freshly grated Parmesan
   cheese
salt and pepper
1 sprig fresh parsley, to garnish

1 Preheat the oven to 200°C/ 400°F/Gas 6. Place the chicken in a blender or food processor and blend until finely minced. Transfer to a bowl.

2 Place the mushrooms, garlic, parsley and tarragon in the food processor and blend until finely minced.

3 Beat the mushroom mixture into the chicken mixture thoroughly, then add the egg, salt and pepper and lemon juice to taste and mix together well.

4 If necessary, cook the cannelloni in plenty of salted boiling water according to the instructions, then drain well on a clean dish towel.

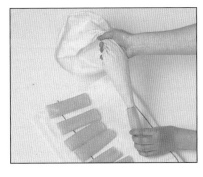

5 Place the filling in a piping bag fitted with a large plain nozzle. Use this to fill each tube of cannelloni once they are cool enough to handle.

6 Lay the filled cannelloni tightly together in a single layer in a buttered shallow ovenproof dish. Spoon over the tomato sauce and sprinkle with Parmesan cheese. Bake in the oven for 30 minutes or until brown and bubbling. Serve garnished with a sprig of parsley.

Koftas in Tomato Sauce

Delicious meatballs in a rich tomato sauce. Serve with pasta and grated Parmesan cheese, if desired.

INGREDIENTS

Serves 4

675g/1¹/₂lb chicken
1 onion, grated
1 garlic clove, crushed
15ml/1 tbsp chopped fresh parsley
2.5ml/¹/₂ tsp ground cumin
2.5ml/¹/₂ tsp ground coriander
1 egg, beaten
seasoned flour, for rolling
50ml/2fl oz/¹/₄ cup olive oil
salt and black pepper
chopped fresh parsley, to garnish

For the tomato sauce
15g/¹/₂oz/1 tbsp butter
15g/¹/₂oz/2 tbsp plain flour
250ml/8fl oz/1 cup chicken stock
400g/14oz can chopped tomatoes, with
  the juice
5ml/1 tsp caster sugar
1.5ml/¹/₄ tsp dried mixed herbs

1 Preheat the oven to 180°C/ 350°F/Gas 4. Remove any skin and bone from the chicken and mince or chop finely.

2 Put into a bowl together with the onion, garlic, parsley, spices, seasoning and beaten egg.

3 Mix together thoroughly and shape into 24 x 4cm/1¹/₂in balls. Roll lightly in seasoned flour.

4 Heat the oil in a frying pan and brown the balls in small batches (this keeps the oil temperature hot and prevents the flour becoming soggy). Remove and drain on kitchen paper. There is no need to cook the balls any further at this stage as they will cook in the tomato sauce.

5 To make the tomato sauce, melt the butter in a large saucepan. Add the flour, and then blend in the stock and tomatoes along with their juice. Add the caster sugar and mixed herbs. Bring to the boil, cover and simmer for 10–15 minutes.

6 Place the browned chicken balls into a shallow ovenproof dish and pour over the tomato sauce, cover with foil and bake in the preheated oven for 30–40 minutes. Adjust the seasoning to taste and sprinkle with parsley.

Tuscan Chicken

*This simple peasant casserole has all
the flavours of traditional Tuscan
ingredients. The wine can be
replaced by chicken stock.*

INGREDIENTS

Serves 4

8 chicken thighs, skinned
5ml/1 tsp olive oil
1 medium onion, thinly sliced
2 red peppers, seeded and sliced
1 garlic clove, crushed
300ml/^{1}/$_2$ pint/1^1/$_4$ cups passata
150ml/^{1}/$_4$ pint/^{2}/$_3$ cup dry white wine
large sprig fresh oregano, or 5ml/1 tsp
    dried oregano
400g/14oz can cannellini beans, drained
45ml/3 tbsp fresh breadcrumbs
salt and black pepper

1 Fry the chicken in the oil in a
non-stick or heavy pan until
golden brown. Remove and keep
hot. Add the onion and peppers to
the pan and gently sauté until softened, but not brown. Stir in the
garlic.

2 Add the chicken, passata, wine
and oregano. Season well,
bring to the boil then cover the
pan tightly.

3 Lower the heat and simmer
gently, stirring occasionally for
30–35 minutes or until the chicken
is tender and the juices run clear,
not pink, when pierced with the
point of a knife.

4 Stir in the cannellini beans and
simmer for a further 5 minutes
until heated through. Sprinkle
with the breadcrumbs and cook
under a hot grill until golden
brown.

Chilli Chicken Couscous

Couscous is a very easy alternative to rice and makes a good base for all kinds of ingredients.

INGREDIENTS

Serves 4

225g/8oz/2 cups couscous

1 litre/1³/4 pints/4 cups boiling water

5ml/1 tsp olive oil

400g/14oz chicken without
  skin and bone, diced

1 yellow pepper, seeded and sliced

2 large courgettes, sliced thickly

1 small green chilli, thinly sliced,
  or 5ml/1 tsp chilli sauce

1 large tomato, diced

425g/15oz can chick-peas, drained

salt and black pepper

coriander or parsley sprigs to garnish

1 Place the couscous in a large bowl and pour over boiling water. Cover and leave to stand for 30 minutes.

2 Heat the oil in a large, non-stick pan and stir-fry the chicken quickly to seal, then reduce the heat.

3 Stir in the pepper, courgettes and chilli or sauce and cook for about 10 minutes, until the vegetables are softened.

4 Stir in the tomato and chick-peas then add the couscous. Adjust the seasoning and stir over a moderate heat until hot. Serve garnished with sprigs of fresh coriander or parsley.

Chicken Bean Bake

Sliced aubergine layered with beans, chicken and topped with yogurt.

INGREDIENTS

Serves 4

1 medium aubergine, thinly sliced

15ml/1 tbsp olive oil, for brushing

450g/1lb boneless chicken breast, diced

1 medium onion, chopped

400g/14oz can chopped tomatoes

425g/15oz can red kidney beans, drained

15ml/1 tbsp paprika

15ml/1 tbsp chopped fresh thyme,
  or 5ml/1 tsp dried

5ml/1 tsp chilli sauce

350g/12oz/1¹/2 cups Greek-style yogurt

2.5ml/¹/2 tsp grated nutmeg

salt and black pepper

1 Preheat the oven to 190°C/375°F/Gas 5. Arrange the aubergine in a colander and sprinkle with salt.

2 Leave the aubergine for 30 minutes, then rinse and pat dry. Brush a non-stick pan with oil and fry the aubergine in batches, turning once, until golden.

3 Remove the aubergine, add the chicken and onion to the pan, and cook until lightly browned. Stir in the tomatoes, beans, paprika, thyme, chilli sauce and seasoning. In a bowl, mix together the yogurt and grated nutmeg.

4 Layer the meat and aubergine in an ovenproof dish, finishing with aubergine. Spread the yogurt evenly over the top and bake for 50–60 minutes, until golden.

Chicken Lasagne

Based on the Italian beef lasagne, this is an excellent dish for entertaining guests of all ages. Serve simply with a green salad.

INGREDIENTS

Serves 8

30ml/2 tbsp olive oil

900g/2lb minced raw chicken

225g/8oz/1¹/₂ cups rindless streaky bacon
    rashers, chopped

2 garlic cloves, crushed

450g/1lb leeks, sliced

225g/8oz/1¹/₄ cups carrots, diced

30ml/2 tbsps tomato purée

475ml/16fl oz/2 cups chicken stock

12 sheets (no need to pre-cook)
    lasagne verde

For the cheese sauce

50g/2oz/4 tbsp butter

50g/2oz/¹/₂ cup plain flour

600ml/1 pint/2¹/₂ cups milk

115g/4oz/1 cup grated mature
    Cheddar cheese

1.5ml/¹/₄ tsp dry English mustard

salt and black pepper

1 Heat the oil in a large flame-proof casserole dish and brown the minced chicken and bacon briskly, separating the pieces with a wooden spoon. Add the crushed garlic cloves, sliced leeks and diced carrots and cook for about 5 minutes until softened. Add the tomato purée, stock and seasoning. Bring to the boil, cover and simmer for 30 minutes.

2 To make the sauce, melt the butter in a saucepan, add the flour and gradually blend in the milk, stirring until smooth. Bring to the boil, stirring all the time until thickened and simmer for several minutes. Add half the grated cheese and the mustard and season to taste.

3 Preheat the oven to 190°C/ 375°F/Gas 5. Layer the chicken mixture, lasagne and half the cheese sauce in a 2.5 litre/5 pint ovenproof dish, starting and finishing with a layer of chicken.

4 Pour the remaining half of the cheese sauce over the top to cover, sprinkle over the remaining cheese and bake in the preheated oven for 1 hour, or until bubbling and lightly browned on top.

Chicken with Herbs and Lentils

Chicken baked on lentils and served topped with garlic butter.

INGREDIENTS

Serves 4

115g/4oz piece of thick bacon or belly
   pork, rind removed, chopped
1 large onion, sliced
475ml/16fl oz/2 cups well-flavoured
   chicken stock
bay leaf
2 sprigs each parsley, marjoram and
  thyme
225g/8oz/1 cup green or brown lentils
4 chicken portions
salt and black pepper
25–50g/1–2oz/2–4 tbsp garlic butter

COOK'S TIP

For economy buy a smallish
chicken and cut it in quarters, to
give generous portions.

1 Fry the bacon gently in a large,
heavy-based flameproof
casserole until all the fat runs out
and the bacon begins to brown.
Add the onion and fry for about
another 2 minutes.

2 Stir in the chicken stock, bay
leaf, herb stalks and some of
the leafy parts (keep some herb
sprigs for garnish), lentils and seasoning. Preheat the oven to
190°C/375°F/ Gas 5.

3 Fry the chicken portions in a
frying pan to brown the skin
before placing on top of the lentils.
Sprinkle with seasoning and some
of the herbs.

4 Cover the casserole and cook
in the oven for about 40
minutes. Serve with a knob of
garlic butter on each portion and a
few of the remaining herb sprigs.

Chicken Bobotie

Perfect for a buffet party, this mild curry dish is set with savoury custard, which makes serving easy. Serve with boiled rice and chutney.

INGREDIENTS

Serves 8

two thick slices white bread

450ml/^{3}/$_4$ pint/1^3/$_4$ cups milk

30ml/2 tbsp olive oil

2 medium onions, finely chopped

45ml/3 tbsp medium curry powder

1.25kg/2^1/$_2$lb minced raw chicken

15ml/1 tbsp apricot jam, chutney or caster
  sugar

30ml/2 tbsp wine vinegar or lemon juice

3 size 4 eggs, beaten

50g/2oz/^{1}/$_3$ cup raisins or sultanas

12 whole almonds

salt and black pepper

3 Mash the bread in the milk and add to the pan with one of the beaten eggs and the raisins.

4 Grease a 1.5 litre/2^1/$_2$ pints/ 6^1/$_4$ cups shallow ovenproof dish with butter. Spoon in the chicken mixture and level the top. Cover with buttered foil and bake in the oven for 30 minutes.

5 Meanwhile, beat the remaining eggs and milk. Remove the dish from the oven and lower the temperature to 150°C/300°F/Gas 2. Break up the meat using a fork and pour over the egg.

6 Scatter the almonds over and bake, uncovered, for 30 minutes until set and brown.

1 Preheat the oven to 180°C/ 350°F/Gas 4. Soak the bread in 150ml/^{1}/$_4$ pint/^{2}/$_3$ cup of the milk. Heat the oil in a frying pan and gently fry the onions until tender, then add the curry powder and cook for a further 2 minutes.

2 Add the minced chicken and brown all over, separating the grains of meat as they brown. Remove from the heat, season with salt and black pepper, add the apricot jam, chutney or caster sugar and the wine vinegar or lemon juice.

Oat-crusted Chicken with Sage

Oats make a good coating for savoury foods, and offer a good way to add extra fibre.

INGREDIENTS

Serves 4

45ml/3 tbsp skimmed milk

10ml/2 tsp English mustard

40g/1$\frac{1}{2}$oz/$\frac{1}{2}$ cup rolled oats

45ml/3 tbsp chopped sage leaves

8 chicken thighs or drumsticks, skinned

115g/4oz/$\frac{1}{2}$ cup low-fat fromage frais

5ml/1 tsp wholegrain mustard

salt and black pepper

fresh sage leaves, to garnish

COOK'S TIP

If fresh sage is not available, choose another fresh herb, such as thyme or parsley, rather than a dried alternative.

1 Preheat the oven to 200°C/400°F/Gas 6. Mix together the milk and English mustard.

2 Mix the oats with 30ml/2 tbsp of the sage and the seasoning on a plate. Brush the chicken with the milk and press into the oats.

3 Place the chicken on a baking sheet and bake for about 40 minutes, or until the juices run clear, not pink, when pierced through the thickest part.

4 Meanwhile, mix together the low-fat fromage frais, wholegrain mustard, remaining sage and seasoning, then serve with the chicken. Garnish the chicken with fresh sage and serve hot or cold.

Chicken Pastitsio

A traditional Greek pastitsio is a rich, high fat dish made with beef mince, but this lighter version with chicken is just as tasty.

INGREDIENTS

Serves 4–6

450g/1lb lean minced chicken

1 large onion, finely chopped

60ml/4 tbsp tomato purée

250ml/8fl oz/1 cup red wine or stock

5ml/1 tsp ground cinnamon

300g/11oz/2^1/$_2$ cups macaroni

300ml/^{1}/$_2$ pint/1^1/$_4$ cups milk

25g/1oz/2 tbsp sunflower margarine

25g/1oz/4 tbsp plain flour

5ml/1 tsp grated nutmeg

2 tomatoes, sliced

60ml/4 tbsp wholemeal breadcrumbs

salt and black pepper

green salad, to serve

1 Preheat the oven to 220°C/ 425°F/Gas 7. Fry the chicken and onion in a non-stick pan without fat, stirring until lightly browned.

2 Stir in the tomato purée, red wine or stock and cinnamon. Season, then cover and simmer for 5 minutes, stirring from time to time. Remove from the heat.

3 Cook the macaroni in plenty of boiling, salted water until just tender, then drain.

4 Layer the macaroni with the meat mixture in a wide ovenproof dish.

5 Place the milk, margarine and flour in a saucepan and whisk over a moderate heat until thickened and smooth. Add the nutmeg, and season to taste.

6 Pour the sauce evenly over the pasta and meat layers. Arrange the tomato slices on top and sprinkle lines of wholemeal bread-crumbs over the surface.

7 Bake for 30–35 minutes, or until golden brown and bubbling. Serve hot with a fresh green salad.

Crunchy Stuffed Chicken Breasts

These can be prepared ahead of time as long as the stuffing is quite cold before the chicken is stuffed. It is an ideal dish for entertaining.

INGREDIENTS

Serves 4

4 chicken breasts, boned

25g/1oz/2 tbsp butter

1 garlic clove, crushed

15ml/1 tbsp Dijon mustard

For the stuffing

15g/^{1}/$_2$ oz/1 tbsp butter

1 bunch spring onions, sliced

45ml/3 tbsp fresh breadcrumbs

25g/1oz/2 tbsp pine nuts

1 egg yolk

15ml/1 tbsp chopped fresh parsley

salt and black pepper

60ml/4 tbsp grated cheese

For the topping

2 bacon rashers, finely chopped

50g/2oz/1 cup fresh breadcrumbs

15ml/1 tbsp grated Parmesan cheese

15ml/1 tbsp chopped fresh parsley

1 Preheat the oven to 200°C/ 400°F/Gas 6. To make the stuffing, heat 15g/^{1}/$_2$ oz/1 tbsp of the butter in a frying pan and cook the spring onions until soft. Remove from the heat and allow to cool for a few minutes.

2 Add the remaining ingredients and mix thoroughly.

3 To make the topping, fry the chopped bacon until crispy, drain and add to the breadcrumbs, Parmesan cheese and fresh parsley.

4 Carefully cut a deep pocket in each of the chicken breasts, using a sharp knife.

5 Divide the stuffing into four and use to fill the pockets. Put in a buttered ovenproof dish.

6 Melt the remaining butter, mix it with the crushed garlic and mustard, and brush liberally over the chicken. Press on the topping and bake uncovered for about 30–40 minutes, or until tender.

Chicken with White Wine and Garlic

*Add the extra garlic to this dish if
you like a stronger flavour.*

INGREDIENTS

Serves 4

1.5kg/3¹/₂lb chicken, cut into serving
 pieces
1 onion, sliced
3–6 garlic cloves, to taste, crushed
5ml/1 tsp dried thyme
475ml/16fl oz/2 cups dry white wine
115g/4oz/1 cup green olives (16–18),
 pitted
1 bay leaf
15ml/1 tbsp lemon juice
15–25g/¹/₂–1oz/1–2 tbsp butter
salt and black pepper

1 Heat a deep, heavy frying pan.
When hot, add the chicken
pieces, skin side down, and cook
over medium heat until browned,
about 10 minutes. Turn and brown
the other side, 5–8 minutes more.

2 Transfer the chicken pieces to
a plate and set aside.

3 Drain the excess fat from the
frying pan, leaving about
15ml/1 tbsp. Add the sliced onion
and 2.5ml/¹/₂ tsp salt and cook
until just soft, about 5 minutes.
Add the garlic and thyme and cook
1 minute more.

4 Add the wine and stir, scraping
up any bits that cling to the
pan. Bring to the boil and boil for
1 minute. Stir in the olives.

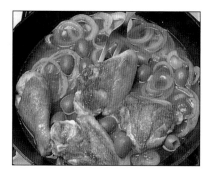

5 Return the chicken pieces to
the pan. Add the bay leaf and
season lightly with pepper. Lower
the heat, cover, and simmer until
the chicken is cooked through,
about 20–30 minutes.

6 Transfer the chicken pieces to a
warmed plate. Stir the lemon
juice into the sauce. Whisk in the
butter to thicken the sauce slightly.
Spoon over the chicken and serve.

Chicken Meat Loaf

*Just slice the loaf up and serve it hot
or cold.*

INGREDIENTS

Serves 4

15ml/1 tbsp olive oil
1 onion, chopped
1 green pepper, seeded and chopped
1 garlic clove, crushed
450g/1lb minced chicken
50g/2oz/1 cup fresh breadcrumbs
1 egg, beaten
50g/2oz/¹/₂ cup pine nuts
12 sun-dried tomatoes in oil, drained and
 chopped
75ml/5 tbsp milk
10ml/2 tsp chopped fresh rosemary, or
 2.5ml/¹/₂ tsp dried rosemary
5ml/1 tsp ground fennel
2.5ml/¹/₂ tsp dried oregano
2.5ml/¹/₂ tsp salt

1 Preheat the oven to 190°C/
375°F/Gas 5. Heat the oil in a
frying pan. Add the onion, green
pepper and garlic and cook over
low heat, stirring often, until just
softened, about 8–10 minutes.
Remove from the heat and allow
to cool.

2 Place the chicken in a large
bowl. Add the onion mixture
and the remaining ingredients and
mix thoroughly together.

3 Transfer to a 21 x 11 cm/8¹/₂ x
4¹/₂in loaf tin, packing the
mixture down firmly. Bake until
golden brown, about 1 hour. Serve
hot or cold in slices.

Stuffed Chicken Wings

These tasty stuffed wings can be served hot or cold at a buffet. They can be prepared and frozen in advance.

INGREDIENTS

Makes 12
12 large chicken wings

For the filling
5ml/1 tsp cornflour
1.5ml/¼ tsp salt
2.5ml/½ tsp fresh thyme
pinch of black pepper

For the coating
225g/8oz/3 cups dried breadcrumbs
30ml/2 tbsp sesame seeds
2 eggs, beaten
oil, for deep-frying

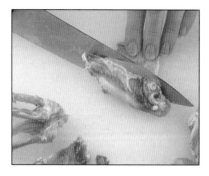

1 Remove the wing tips and discard or use them for making stock. Skin the second joint sections, removing the two small bones and reserve the meat for the filling.

2 Mince the reserved meat and mix with the filling ingredients.

3 Holding the large end of the bone on the third section of the wing and using a sharp knife, cut the skin and flesh away from the bone, scraping down and pulling the meat over the small end forming a pocket. Repeat this process with the remaining wing sections.

4 Fill the tiny pockets with the filling. Mix the dried breadcrumbs and the sesame seeds together. Place the breadcrumb mixture and the beaten egg in separate dishes.

5 Brush the meat with beaten egg and roll in breadcrumbs to cover. Chill and repeat to give a second layer, forming a thick coating. Chill until ready to fry.

6 Preheat the oven to 180°C/350°F/Gas 4. Heat 5cm/2in of oil in a heavy-based pan until hot but not smoking or the breadcrumbs will burn. Gently fry two or three wings at a time until golden brown, remove and drain on kitchen paper. Complete the cooking in the preheated oven for 15–20 minutes or until tender.

Chicken Paella

*There are many variations of this
basic recipe. Any seasonal vegetables
can be added, together with mussels
and other shellfish. Serve straight
from the pan.*

INGREDIENTS

Serves 4

4 chicken legs (thighs and drumsticks)

60ml/4 tbsp olive oil

1 large onion, finely chopped

1 garlic clove, crushed

5ml/1 tsp ground turmeric

115g/4oz chorizo sausage or smoked ham

225g/8oz/generous 1 cup long grain rice

600ml/1 pint/2^1/$_2$ cups chicken stock

4 tomatoes, skinned, seeded and chopped

1 red pepper, seeded and sliced

115g/4oz/1 cup frozen peas

salt and black pepper

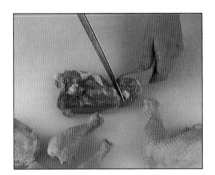

1 Preheat the oven to 180°C/
350°F/Gas 4. Cut the chicken
legs in half.

2 Heat the oil in a 30cm/12in
paella pan or large flameproof
casserole and brown the chicken
pieces on both sides. Add the
onion and garlic and stir in the
turmeric. Cook for 2 minutes.

3 Slice the sausage or dice the
ham and add to the pan, with
the rice and stock. Bring to the boil
and season to taste, cover and bake
for 15 minutes.

4 Remove from the oven and
add the chopped tomatoes and
sliced red pepper and frozen peas.
Return to the oven and cook for a
further 10–15 minutes or until the
chicken is tender and the rice has
absorbed the stock.

Apricot and Chicken Casserole

A mild curry and fruity chicken dish served with almond rice. Makes a good winter meal.

Serves 4

15ml/1 tbsp oil

8 chicken thighs, boned and skinned

1 medium onion, finely chopped

5ml/1 tsp medium curry powder

30ml/2 tbsp plain flour

450ml/^{3}/4 pint/1^7/8 cups chicken
  stock

juice of 1 large orange

8 dried apricots, halved

15ml/1 tbsp sultanas

salt and black pepper

For the almond rice

225g/8oz/2 cups cooked long grain rice

15g/^{1}/2oz/1 tbsp butter

50g/2oz/^{1}/2 cup toasted, flaked almonds

1 Preheat the oven to 190°C/
375°F/Gas 5. Heat the oil in a
large frying pan. Cut the chicken
into cubes and brown quickly all
over in the oil. Add the chopped
onion and cook gently until soft
and lightly browned.

2 Transfer the chicken and onion
to a large flameproof casserole
and sprinkle in the curry powder
and cook again for a few minutes.
Add the flour and blend in the
stock and orange juice. Bring to
the boil and season with salt and
freshly ground black pepper.

3 Add the apricots and sultanas,
cover with a lid and cook
gently for an hour, or until tender,
in the preheated oven. Adjust the
seasoning to taste.

4 To make the almond rice,
reheat the pre-cooked rice
with the butter and season to taste.
Stir in the toasted almonds just
before serving.

Stoved Chicken

"Stoved" is derived from the French étouffer – to cook in a covered pot – and originates from the Franco/Scottish "Alliance" of the seventeenth century.

INGREDIENTS

Serves 4

1kg/2¼lb potatoes, cut into 5mm/¼in slices

2 large onions, thinly sliced

15ml/1 tbsp chopped fresh thyme

25g/1oz/2 tbsp butter

15ml/1 tbsp oil

2 large slices bacon, chopped

4 large chicken joints, halved

bay leaf

600ml/1 pint/2½ cups chicken stock

salt and black pepper

1 Preheat the oven to 150°C/ 300°F/Gas 2. Make a thick layer of half the potato slices in the bottom of a large, heavy casserole, then cover with half the onion. Sprinkle with half the thyme, and seasonings.

2 Heat the butter and oil in a large frying pan, then brown the bacon and chicken.

3 Using a slotted spoon, transfer the chicken and bacon to the casserole. Reserve the fat in the pan. Sprinkle the remaining thyme, bay leaf and some seasoning over the chicken, then cover with the remaining onion, followed by a neat layer of overlapping potato slices. Sprinkle with seasoning.

4 Pour the stock into the casserole, brush the potatoes with the reserved fat, then cover tightly and cook in the oven for about 2 hours, until the chicken is tender.

5 Preheat the grill. Uncover the casserole and place under the grill and cook until the slices of potato are beginning to brown and crisp. Serve hot.

SALADS,
BARBECUES &
GRILLS

~

Coronation Chicken

A summer favourite – serve with a crisp green salad.

Serves 8

$^1/_2$ lemon

2.25kg/5–5$^1/_4$lb chicken

1 onion, quartered

1 carrot, quartered

large bouquet garni

8 black peppercorns, crushed

salt

watercress sprigs, to garnish

For the sauce

1 small onion, chopped

15g/$^1/_2$oz/1 tbsp butter

15ml/1 tbsp curry paste

15ml/1 tbsp tomato purée

120ml/4fl oz/$^1/_2$ cup red wine

bay leaf

juice of $^1/_2$ lemon, or more to taste

10–15ml/2–3 tsp apricot jam

300ml/$^1/_2$ pint/1$^1/_4$ cups mayonnaise

120ml/4fl oz/$^1/_2$ cup whipping cream,
   whipped

salt and black pepper

1 Put the lemon half in the chicken cavity, then place the chicken in a saucepan that it just fits. Add the vegetables, bouquet garni, peppercorns and salt.

2 Add sufficient water to come two-thirds of the way up the chicken, bring to the boil, then cover and cook gently for 1$^1/_2$ hours, until the juices run clear.

3 Transfer the chicken to a large bowl, pour over the cooking liquid and leave to cool. Skin, bone, then chop the chicken flesh.

4 To make the sauce, cook the onion in the butter until soft. Add the curry paste, tomato purée, wine, bay leaf and lemon juice, then cook for 10 minutes. Add the apricot jam; sieve and cool.

5 Beat the sauce into the mayonnaise. Fold in the cream; add seasoning, then stir in the chicken and garnish with watercress.

Warm Stir-fried Salad

Warm salads are becoming increasingly popular because they are delicious and nutritious. Arrange the salad leaves on four individual plates, so the hot stir-fry can be served straight from the wok, ensuring the lettuce remains crisp and the chicken warm.

INGREDIENTS

Serves 4

15ml/1 tbsp fresh tarragon

2 chicken breasts, about 225g/8oz each,
   boned and skinned

5cm/2in piece fresh root ginger, peeled
   and finely chopped

45ml/3 tbsp light soy sauce

15ml/1 tbsp sugar

15ml/1 tbsp sunflower oil

1 head Chinese lettuce

1/2 frisée lettuce, torn into bite-size
   pieces

115g/4oz/1 cup unsalted cashew nuts

2 large carrots, peeled and cut into fine
   strips

salt and black pepper

1 Chop the fresh tarragon. Cut the chicken into fine strips and place in a bowl.

2 To make the marinade, mix together in a bowl the tarragon, ginger, soy sauce, sugar and seasoning.

3 Pour the marinade over the chicken strips and leave to marinate for 2–4 hours.

4 Strain the chicken from the marinade, reserving the liquid. Heat a wok or large frying pan, then add the oil. When the oil is hot, stir-fry the chicken for 3 minutes, add the marinade and bubble for 2–3 minutes.

5 Slice the Chinese lettuce and arrange on a plate with the frisée. Toss the cashews and carrots together with the chicken and sauce, pile on top of the bed of lettuce and serve immediately.

Fusilli with Chicken, Tomatoes and Broccoli

This is a really hearty main-course salad for a hungry family.

Serves 4

675g/1¹/2lb ripe but firm plum tomatoes, quartered

90ml/6 tbsp olive oil

5ml/1 tsp dried oregano

salt and black pepper

350g/12oz broccoli florets

1 small onion, sliced

5ml/1 tsp dried thyme

450g/1lb/3 cups chicken breast, boned, skinned and cubed

3 garlic cloves, crushed

15ml/1 tbsp fresh lemon juice

450g/1lb fusilli pasta

1 Preheat the oven to 200°C/ 400°F/Gas 6.

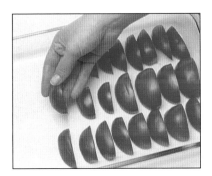

2 Place the tomatoes in a baking dish. Add 15ml/1 tbsp of the oil, the oregano, and 5ml/¹/2 tsp salt and stir to blend.

3 Bake until the tomatoes are just browned, about 30–40 minutes; do not stir.

4 Meanwhile, bring a large pan of salted water to the boil. Add the broccoli and cook until just tender, about 5 minutes. Drain and set aside. (Alternatively, steam the broccoli until tender.)

5 Heat 30ml/2 tbsp of the oil in a large non-stick frying pan. Add the onion, thyme, chicken cubes and 2.5ml/¹/2 tsp salt. Cook over high heat, stirring often, until the meat is cooked and beginning to brown, 5–7 minutes. Add the garlic and cook 1 minute more, stirring.

6 Remove from the heat. Stir in the lemon juice and season with pepper. Keep warm until the pasta is cooked.

7 Bring another large pan of salted water to the boil. Add the fusilli and cook until just tender (check the instructions on the packet for timing). Drain and place in a large bowl. Toss with the remaining oil.

8 Add the broccoli to the chicken mixture. Add to the fusilli. Add the tomatoes and stir gently to blend. Serve immediately.

Chinese-style Chicken Salad

Shredded chicken is served with a tasty peanut sauce.

INGREDIENTS

Serves 4

4 boneless chicken breasts, about
   175g/6oz each
60ml/4 tbsp dark soy sauce
pinch of Chinese five-spice powder
a good squeeze of lemon juice
$1/2$ cucumber, peeled and cut into
   matchsticks
5ml/1 tsp salt
45ml/3 tbsp sunflower oil
30ml/2 tbsp sesame oil
15ml/1 tbsp sesame seeds
30ml/2 tbsp dry sherry
2 carrots, cut into matchsticks
8 spring onions, shredded
75g/3oz/$1/2$ cup beansprouts

For the sauce
60ml/4 tbsp crunchy peanut butter
10ml/2 tsp lemon juice
10ml/2 tsp sesame oil
1.5ml/$1/4$ tsp hot chilli powder
1 spring onion, finely chopped

1 Put the chicken portions into a large pan and just cover with water. Add 15ml/1 tbsp of the soy sauce, the Chinese five-spice powder and lemon juice, cover and bring to the boil, then simmer for about 20 minutes.

2 Place the cucumber matchsticks in a colander, sprinkle with the salt and cover with a weighted plate. Leave to drain for 30 minutes.

3 Heat the oils in a large frying pan or wok. Add the sesame seeds, fry for 30 seconds and then stir in the remaining soy sauce and the sherry. Add the carrots and stir-fry for 2–3 minutes. Remove and reserve.

4 Remove the chicken from the pan and leave until cool enough to handle. Discard the skins and bash the chicken lightly with a rolling pin to loosen the fibres. Slice in strips and reserve.

5 Rinse the cucumber well, pat dry with kitchen paper and place in a bowl. Add the spring onions, beansprouts, cooked carrots, pan juices and shredded chicken, and mix together. Transfer to a shallow dish. Cover and chill for about 1 hour, turning the mixture in the juices once or twice.

6 To make the sauce, cream the peanut butter with the lemon juice, sesame oil and chilli powder, adding a little hot water to form a paste, then stir in the spring onion. Arrange the chicken mixture on a serving dish and serve with the peanut butter.

Maryland Salad

Barbecue-grilled chicken, sweetcorn, bacon, banana and watercress combine here in a sensational main-course salad. Serve with jacket potatoes and a knob of butter.

INGREDIENTS

Serves 4

4 chicken breasts, boned

225g/8oz rindless unsmoked bacon

4 corn on the cob

45ml/3 tbsp butter, softened

4 ripe bananas, peeled and halved

4 firm tomatoes, halved

1 escarole or butterhead lettuce

1 bunch watercress

salt and black pepper

For the dressing

75ml/5 tbsp groundnut oil

15ml/1 tbsp white wine vinegar

10ml/2 tsp maple syrup

10ml/2 tsp mild mustard

1 Season the chicken breasts, brush with oil and barbecue or grill for 15 minutes, turning once. Barbecue or grill the bacon for 8–10 minutes, or until crisp.

2 Bring a large saucepan of salted water to the boil. Shuck and trim the corn cobs. Boil for 20 minutes. For extra flavour, brush with butter and brown over the barbecue or under the grill. Barbecue or grill the bananas and tomatoes for 6–8 minutes, brush these with butter too if you wish.

3 To make the dressing, combine the oil, vinegar, maple syrup and mustard with seasoning and 15ml/1 tbsp water in a screw-top jar and shake well.

4 Wash, spin thoroughly and dress the salad leaves.

5 Distribute the salad leaves among 4 large plates. Slice the chicken and arrange over the leaves with the bacon, banana, sweetcorn and tomatoes.

Chicken Liver, Bacon and Tomato Salad

Warm salads are especially welcome during the autumn months when the evenings are growing shorter and cooler. Try this rich salad with sweet spinach and bitter leaves of frisée lettuce.

INGREDIENTS

Serves 4

225g/8oz young spinach, stems removed

1 frisée lettuce

105ml/7 tbsp groundnut or sunflower oil

175g/6oz rindless unsmoked bacon, cut into strips

75g/3oz day-old bread, crusts removed and cut into short fingers

450g/1lb chicken livers

115g/4oz cherry tomatoes

salt and black pepper

1 Place the salad leaves in a salad bowl. Heat 60ml/4 tbsp of the oil in a large frying pan. Add the bacon and cook for 3–4 minutes or until crisp and brown. Remove the bacon with a slotted spoon and drain on a piece of kitchen paper.

2 To make the croûtons, fry the bread in the bacon-flavoured oil, tossing until crisp and golden. Drain on kitchen paper.

3 Heat the remaining 45ml/3 tbsp of oil in the frying pan, add the chicken livers and fry briskly for 2–3 minutes. Turn out over the salad leaves, add the bacon, croûtons and tomatoes. Season, toss and serve.

Chicken Satay

Marinate in the satay sauce overnight to allow the flavours to penetrate the chicken. Soak wooden skewers in water overnight to prevent them from burning while cooking.

INGREDIENTS

Serves 4

4 chicken breasts
lemon slices, to garnish
lettuce leaves, to serve
spring onions, to serve

For the satay

115g/4oz/^{1}/$_2$ cup crunchy peanut butter
1 small onion, chopped
1 garlic clove, crushed
30ml/2 tbsp chutney
60ml/4 tbsp olive oil
5ml/1 tsp light soy sauce
30ml/2 tbsp lemon juice
1.5ml/^{1}/$_4$ tsp chilli powder or cayenne
    pepper

1 Put all the satay ingredients into a food processor or blender and process until smooth. Spoon into a large dish.

2 Remove all bone and skin from the chicken and cut into 2.5cm/1in cubes. Add to the satay mixture and stir to coat the chicken pieces. Cover with clear film and chill for at least 4 hours or, better still, overnight.

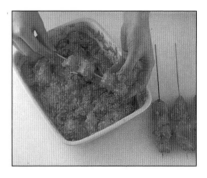

3 Preheat the grill or barbecue. Thread the chicken pieces on to the satay sticks.

4 Cook for 10 minutes, brushing occasionally with the satay sauce. Serve on a bed of lettuce with spring onions and garnish with lemon slices.

Minty Yogurt Chicken

Chicken marinated with yogurt, mint, lemon and honey and grilled.

INGREDIENTS

Serves 4

8 chicken thigh portions, skinned

15ml/1 tbsp clear honey

30ml/2 tbsp lime or lemon juice

30ml/2 tbsp natural yogurt

60ml/4 tbsp chopped fresh mint

salt and black pepper

new potatoes and a tomato salad,
    to serve

1 Slash the chicken flesh at regular intervals with a sharp knife. Place in a bowl.

2 Mix together the honey, lime or lemon juice, yogurt, seasoning and half the mint.

3 Spoon the marinade over the chicken and leave to marinate for 30 minutes. Line the grill pan with foil and cook the chicken under a moderately hot grill until thoroughly cooked and golden brown, turning the chicken occasionally during cooking.

4 Sprinkle with the remaining mint and serve with the potatoes and tomato salad.

Caribbean Chicken Kebabs

These kebabs have a rich, sunshine Caribbean flavour and the marinade keeps them moist without the need for oil. Serve with a colourful salad and rice.

INGREDIENTS

Serves 4

500g/1¼lb chicken breasts, boned and
    skinned
finely grated rind of 1 lime
30ml/2 tbsp lime juice
15ml/1 tbsp rum or sherry
15ml/1 tbsp light muscovado sugar
5ml/1 tsp ground cinnamon
2 mangoes, peeled and cubed
rice and salad, to serve

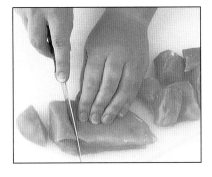

1 Cut the chicken breasts into bite-size chunks and place in a bowl with the grated lime rind and juice, rum or sherry, sugar and cinnamon. Toss well, cover and leave to marinate for 1 hour.

COOK'S TIP

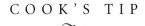

The rum or sherry adds a lovely rich flavour, but it is optional so can be omitted if you prefer to make the dish more economical.

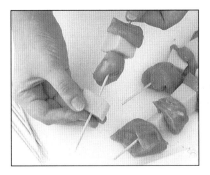

2 Save the juices and thread the chicken on to four wooden skewers, alternating with the mango cubes.

3 Cook the skewers under a hot grill or barbecue for 8–10 minutes, turning occasionally and basting with the reserved juices, until the chicken is tender and golden brown. Serve at once with rice and salad.

Chicken with Pineapple

This chicken has a delicate tang and is very tender. The pineapple not only tenderises the chicken but also gives it a slight sweetness.

INGREDIENTS

Serves 6

225g/8oz can pineapple chunks
5ml/1 tsp ground cumin
5ml/1 tsp ground coriander
2.5ml/^{1}/$_2$ tsp crushed garlic
5ml/1 tsp chilli powder
5ml/1 tsp salt
30ml/2 tbsp natural yogurt
15ml/1 tbsp chopped fresh coriander
orange food colouring (optional)
275g/10oz chicken, skinned and boned
^{1}/$_2$ red pepper
^{1}/$_2$ yellow or green pepper
1 large onion
6 cherry tomatoes
15ml/1 tbsp vegetable oil

1 Drain the pineapple juice into a bowl. Reserve 8 large chunks of pineapple and squeeze the juice from the remaining chunks into the bowl and set aside. You should have about 120ml/4fl oz/^{1}/$_2$ cup pineapple juice.

2 In a large mixing bowl, blend together the cumin, ground coriander, garlic, chilli powder, salt, yogurt, fresh coriander and a few drops of food colouring, if using. Pour in the reserved pineapple juice and mix together.

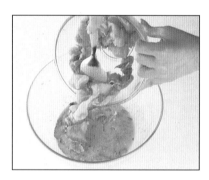

3 Cut the chicken into bite-size cubes, add to the mixing bowl with the yogurt and spice mixture and leave to marinate for about 1–1^1/$_2$ hours.

4 Cut the peppers and onion into bite-size chunks.

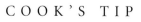

COOK'S TIP

If possible, use a mixture of chicken breast and thigh meat for this recipe.

5 Preheat the grill to medium. Arrange the chicken pieces, peppers, onion, tomatoes and reserved pineapple chunks alternately on 6 wooden or metal skewers.

6 Baste the kebabs with the oil, then place the skewers on a flameproof dish or grill pan. Grill, turning and basting the chicken pieces with the marinade regularly, for about 15 minutes.

7 Once the chicken pieces are cooked, remove them from the grill and serve either with salad or plain boiled rice.

Chicken Breasts with Tomato-Corn Salsa

This hot tomato salsa is good with any grilled or barbecued meats.

Serves 4

4 chicken breast halves, about 175g/6oz
 each, boned and skinned
30ml/2 tbsp fresh lemon juice
30ml/2 tbsp olive oil
10ml/2 tsp ground cumin
10ml/2 tsp dried oregano
15ml/1 tbsp coarse black pepper
salt

For the salsa

1 fresh hot green chilli pepper
450g/1lb tomatoes, seeded and chopped
250g/9oz/1$^{1}/_{4}$ cups sweetcorn, freshly
 cooked or thawed frozen
3 spring onions, chopped
15ml/1 tbsp chopped fresh parsley
30ml/2 tbsp chopped fresh coriander
30ml/2 tbsp fresh lemon juice
45ml/3 tbsp olive oil
5ml/1 tsp salt

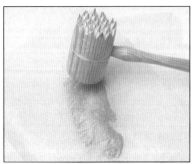

1 With a meat mallet, pound the chicken breasts between two sheets of clear film until thin.

2 In a shallow dish, combine the lemon juice, oil, cumin, oregano and pepper.

3 Add the chicken and turn to coat. Cover and leave to stand for at least 2 hours, or chill overnight.

4 To make the salsa, char the chilli skin either over a gas flame or under the grill. Leave to cool for 5 minutes. Wearing rubber gloves, carefully rub off the charred skin. For a less hot flavour, discard the seeds.

5 Chop the chilli very finely and place in a bowl. Add the remaining salsa ingredients and mix well.

6 Remove the chicken from the marinade. Season lightly.

7 Heat a ridged grill pan. Add the chicken breasts and cook until browned, about 3 minutes. Turn and cook for 3–4 minutes more. Serve with the chilli salsa.

Barbecued Jerk Chicken

Jerk refers to the blend of herb and spice seasoning rubbed into meat, before it is roasted over charcoal sprinkled with pimiento berries. In Jamaica, jerk seasoning was originally used only for pork, but jerked chicken is equally good.

INGREDIENTS

Serves 4

8 chicken pieces

For the marinade

5ml/1 tsp ground allspice

5ml/1 tsp ground cinnamon

5ml/1 tsp dried thyme

1.5ml/$^1/_4$ tsp freshly grated nutmeg

10ml/2 tsp demerara sugar

2 garlic cloves, crushed

15ml/1 tbsp finely chopped onion

15ml/1 tbsp chopped spring onion

15ml/1 tbsp vinegar

30ml/2 tbsp oil

15ml/1 tbsp lime juice

1 hot chilli pepper, chopped

salt and black pepper

salad leaves, to serve

1 Combine all the marinade ingredients in a small bowl. Using a fork, mash them together well to form a thick paste.

2 Lay the chicken pieces on a plate or board and make several lengthways slits in the flesh. Rub the seasoning all over the chicken and into the slits.

3 Place the chicken pieces in a dish, cover with clear film and marinate overnight in the fridge. Shake off any excess seasoning from the chicken. Brush with oil and place either on a baking sheet if cooking inside or on a barbecue grill if barbecuing.

4 Cook under a preheated grill for 45 minutes, turning often. Or, if barbecuing, light the coals and when ready, cook over the coals for 30 minutes, turning often. Serve hot with salad leaves.

COOK'S TIP
~
The flavour is best if you marinate the chicken overnight.

Grilled Chicken

The flavour of the dish, known in Indonesia as Ayam Bakur, *will be more intense if the chicken is marinated overnight. It is an ideal recipe for a party, because the final grilling, barbecuing or baking can be done at the last minute.*

INGREDIENTS

Serves 4

1.5kg/3–3¹/₂lb chicken

4 garlic cloves, crushed

2 lemon grass stems, lower 2 inch sliced

1 teaspoon ground turmeric

475ml/16fl oz/2 cups water

3–4 bay leaves

45ml/3 tbsp each dark and light soy sauce

50g/2oz/¹/₄ cup butter or margarine

salt

boiled rice, to serve

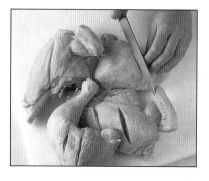

1 Cut the chicken into 4 or 8 portions. Slash the fleshy part of each portion twice and set aside.

2 Grind the garlic, sliced lemon grass, turmeric and salt together into a paste in a food processor or with a mortar and pestle. Rub the paste into the chicken pieces and leave for at least 30 minutes. Wear rubber gloves for this, as the turmeric will stain heavily; or wash your hands immediately after mixing, if you prefer.

3 Transfer the chicken to a wok and pour in the water. Add the bay leaves and bring to a boil. Cover and cook gently for 30 minutes, adding a little more water if necessary and stirring from time to time.

4 Just before serving, add the two soy sauces to the pan together with the butter or margarine.

5 Cook until the chicken is well-coated and the sauce has almost been absorbed. Transfer the chicken to a preheated grill or barbecue, or an oven preheated to 200°C/400°F/Gas 6, to complete the cooking. Cook for a further 10–15 minutes, turning the pieces often so they become golden brown all over. Take care not to let them burn. Baste with remaining sauce during cooking. Serve with boiled rice.

Mediterranean Chicken Skewers

These skewers are easy to assemble, and can be cooked on a grill or charcoal barbecue.

INGREDIENTS

Serves 4

90ml/6 tbsp olive oil

45ml/3 tbsp fresh lemon juice

1 clove garlic, finely chopped

30ml/2 tbsp chopped fresh basil

2 medium courgettes

1 long thin aubergine

300g/11oz boneless chicken, cut into
    5cm/2in cubes

12–16 pickled onions

1 pepper, red or yellow, cut into
    5cm/2in squares

salt and black pepper

1 In a small bowl mix the oil with the lemon juice, garlic and basil. Season with salt and pepper.

2 Slice the courgettes and aubergine lengthways into strips 5mm/¼in thick. Cut them crossways about two-thirds of the way along their length. Discard the shorter length. Wrap half the chicken pieces with the courgette slices, and the other half with the aubergine slices.

3 Prepare the skewers by alternating the chicken, onions and pepper pieces. Lay the prepared skewers on a platter, and sprinkle with the flavoured oil. Leave to marinate for at least 30 minutes. Preheat the grill, or prepare a barbecue.

4 Grill or barbecue for about 10 minutes, or until the vegetables are tender, turning the skewers occasionally. Serve hot.

ROASTS
& PIES

Traditional Roast Chicken

Serve with bacon rolls, chipolata sausages, gravy and stuffing balls.

INGREDIENTS

Serves 4

1.75kg/4lb chicken

streaky bacon rashers

25g/1oz/2 tbsp butter

salt and black pepper

Prune and nut stuffing

25g/1oz/2 tbsp butter

50g/2oz/^{1}/$_2$ cup chopped stoned
    prunes

50g/2oz/^{1}/$_2$ cup chopped walnuts

50g/2oz/1 cup fresh breadcrumbs

1 egg, beaten

15ml/1 tbsp chopped fresh parsley

15ml/1 tbsp chopped fresh chives

30ml/2 tbsp sherry or Port

For the gravy

30ml/2 tbsp plain flour

300ml/^{1}/$_2$ pint/1^1/$_4$ cups chicken stock

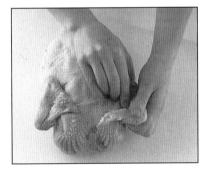

1 Preheat the oven to 190°C/
375°F/Gas 5. Mix all the
stuffing ingredients together in a
bowl and season well.

2 Stuff the neck end of the
chicken quite loosely, allowing
room for the breadcrumbs to swell
during cooking. (Any remaining
stuffing can be shaped into balls
and fried to accompany the roast.)

3 Tuck the neck skin under the
bird to secure the stuffing and
hold in place with the wing tips or
sew with strong thread or fine
string.

4 Place in a roasting tin and
cover the breast with the bacon
rashers. Spread with the remaining
butter, cover loosely with foil and
roast for about 1^1/$_2$ hours. Baste
with the juices in the roasting tin
3 or 4 times during cooking.

5 Remove any trussing string and
transfer to a serving plate,
cover with foil and leave to stand
while making the gravy. (This
standing time allows the flesh to
relax and makes carving easier.)

6 Spoon off the fat from the
juices in the roasting tin. Blend
the flour into the juices and cook
gently until golden brown. Add the
stock, bring to the boil, stirring
until thickened. Adjust the seasoning and strain into a jug to serve.

Roast Chicken with Fennel

In Italy this dish is prepared with wild fennel. Cultivated fennel bulb works just as well.

INGREDIENTS

Serves 4–5

1.6kg/3¹/2lb roasting chicken

1 onion, quartered

100ml/4fl oz/¹/2 cup olive oil

2 medium fennel bulbs

1 clove garlic, peeled

pinch of grated nutmeg

3–4 thin slices pancetta or bacon

100ml/4fl oz/¹/2 cup dry white wine

salt and black pepper

1 Preheat the oven to 180°C/ 350°F/Gas 4. Sprinkle the chicken cavity with salt and pepper. Place the onion quarters in the cavity. Rub the chicken with about 45ml/3 tbsp of the olive oil. Place in a roasting tin.

2 Cut the green fronds from the tops of the fennel bulbs. Chop the fronds together with the garlic. Place in a small bowl and mix with the nutmeg and seasoning.

3 Sprinkle the fennel mixture over the chicken, pressing it on to the oiled skin. Cover the breast with the slices of pancetta or bacon. Sprinkle with 30ml/2 tbsp of the oil. Place in the oven and roast for 30 minutes.

4 Meanwhile, boil or steam the fennel bulbs until barely tender. Remove from the heat and cut into quarters or sixths lengthways. After the chicken has been cooking for 30 minutes, remove the pan from the oven. Baste the chicken with any oils in the pan.

5 Arrange the fennel pieces around the chicken. Sprinkle the fennel with the remaining oil. Pour about half the wine over the chicken, and return to the oven.

6 After 30 minutes more, baste the chicken again. Pour on the remaining wine. Cook for 15–20 minutes. To test, prick the thigh with a fork. If the juices run clear, the chicken is cooked. Serve the chicken surrounded by the fennel.

Chicken with Ham and Cheese

This tasty combination comes from Emilia-Romagna, where it is also prepared with veal.

INGREDIENTS

Serves 4

4 small chicken breasts, skinned and boned

flour seasoned with salt and freshly ground black pepper, for dredging

50g/2oz/4 tbsp butter

3–4 leaves fresh sage

4 thin slices prosciutto crudo, or cooked ham, cut in half

50g/2oz/¹/2 cup freshly grated Parmesan cheese

1 Cut each breast in half lengthways to make two flat fillets of approximately the same thickness. Dredge the chicken in the seasoned flour, and shake off the excess.

2 Preheat the grill. Heat the butter in a large heavy frying pan and add the sage leaves. Add the chicken, in one layer, and cook over low to moderate heat until golden brown on both sides, turning as necessary. This will take about 15 minutes.

3 Remove the chicken from the heat, and arrange on a flameproof serving dish or grill pan. Place one piece of ham on each chicken fillet and top with the grated Parmesan. Grill for 3–4 minutes, or until the cheese has melted. Serve at once.

Pot-roast Chicken with Sausage Stuffing

These casseroled chickens will be tender and succulent.

INGREDIENTS

Serves 6

2 x 1.12kg/2^1/2lb chickens

30ml/2 tbsp vegetable oil

350ml/12fl oz/1^1/2 cups chicken stock or
   half wine and half stock

1 bay leaf

For the stuffing

450g/1lb sausagemeat

1 small onion, chopped

1–2 garlic cloves, finely chopped

5ml/1 tsp hot paprika

2.5ml/^{1}/2 tsp dried chilli (optional)

2.5ml/^{1}/2 tsp dried thyme

1.5ml/^{1}/4 tsp ground allspice

40g/1^1/2oz/1 cup coarse fresh breadcrumbs

1 egg, beaten to mix

salt and black pepper

1 Preheat the oven to 180°C/
350°F/Gas 4 oven.

2 For the stuffing, put the
sausagemeat, onion and garlic
in a frying pan and fry over moderate heat until the sausagemeat is
lightly browned and crumbly, stirring and turning so it cooks evenly.
Remove from the heat and mix in
the remaining stuffing ingredients
with salt and pepper to taste.

3 Divide the stuffing between the
chickens, packing it into the
body cavities (or, if preferred, stuff
the neck end and bake the leftover
stuffing in a separate dish). Truss
the birds.

4 Heat the oil in a flameproof
casserole just big enough to
hold the chickens. Brown the birds
all over.

5 Add the stock and bay leaf and
season. Cover and bring to the
boil, then transfer to the oven. Pot-
roast for 1^1/4 hours or until the
birds are cooked (the juices will
run clear).

6 Untruss the chickens and
spoon the stuffing on to a
serving platter. Arrange the birds
and serve with the strained
cooking liquid.

VARIATION

For Pot-roast Guinea Fowl, use 2
guinea fowl instead of chickens.

Poussins Waldorf

Sunday roast and stuffing, with a difference.

Serves 6

6 poussins, each weighing about
 500g/1¹/4lb
salt and black pepper
40–50g/1¹/2–2oz/3–4 tbsp butter, melted

For the stuffing
25g/1oz/2 tbsp butter
1 onion, finely chopped
300g/11oz/2¹/4 cups cooked rice
2 celery sticks, finely chopped
2 red apples, cored and finely diced
50g/2oz/¹/3 cup walnuts, chopped
75ml/5 tbsp cream sherry or apple juice
30ml/2 tbsp lemon juice

1 Preheat the oven to 180°C/
350°F/Gas 4. To make the
stuffing, melt the butter in a small
frying pan and fry the onion,
stirring occasionally, until soft. Tip
the onion and butter into a bowl
and add the remaining stuffing
ingredients. Season with salt and
pepper and mix well.

2 Divide the stuffing among the
poussins, stuffing the body
cavities. Truss the birds and
arrange in a roasting tin. Sprinkle
with salt and pepper and drizzle
over the melted butter.

3 Roast for about 1¹/4–1¹/2 hours.
Untruss before serving.

CARVING POULTRY

Carving a bird neatly for serving makes the presenta-
tion attractive. You will need a sharp long-bladed
knife, or an electric knife, plus a long 2-pronged fork
and a carving board with a well to catch the juices.

Cut away any trussing string. For a stuffed bird,
spoon the stuffing from the cavity into a serving
dish. For easier carving, remove the wishbone.

Insert the fork into one breast to hold the bird
steady. Cut through the skin to the ball and socket
joint on that side of the body, then slice through it to
sever the leg from the body. Repeat on the other side.

1 Slice through the ball and socket joint in each leg
to sever the thigh and drumstick. If carving
turkey, slice the meat off the thigh and drumstick,
parallel to the bone, turning to get even slices; leave
chicken thighs and drumsticks whole.

2 To carve the breast of a turkey or chicken, cut
5mm/¹/4in thick slices at an angle, slicing down
on both sides of the breastbone. For smaller birds,
remove the meat on each side of the breastbone in a
single piece, then slice across.

Chicken, Leek and Parsley Pie

The flavours of chicken and leek complement each other wonderfully.

INGREDIENTS

Serves 4–6

For the pastry

275g/10oz/2^1/2 cups plain flour

pinch of salt

200g/7oz/^{7}/8 cup butter, diced

2 egg yolks

For the filling

3 part-boned chicken breasts

flavouring ingredients e.g. bouquet garni
   black peppercorns, onion and carrot

50g/2oz/4 tbsp butter

2 leeks, thinly sliced

50g/2oz/^{1}/2 cup Cheddar cheese, grated

25g/1oz/^{1}/3 cup Parmesan cheese, finely
   grated

45ml/3 tbsp chopped fresh parsley

30ml/2 tbsp wholegrain mustard

5ml/1 tsp cornflour

300ml/^{1}/2 pint/1^1/4 cups double cream

salt and black pepper

beaten egg, to glaze

mixed green salad, to serve

1 To make the pastry, first sift the flour and salt. Blend together the butter and egg yolks in a food processor until creamy. Add the flour and process until the mixture is just coming together. Add about 15ml/1 tbsp cold water and process for a few seconds more. Turn out on to a lightly floured surface and knead lightly. Wrap in clear film and chill for about 1 hour.

2 Meanwhile, poach the chicken breasts in water to cover, with the flavouring ingredients added. Cook the chicken until tender. Leave to cool in the liquid.

3 Preheat the oven to 200°C/ 400°F/Gas 6. Divide the pastry into two pieces, one slightly larger than the other. Roll out the larger piece on a lightly floured surface and use to line an 18 x 28cm/7 x 11in baking dish or tin. Prick the base with a fork and bake for 15 minutes. Leave to cool.

4 Lift the cooled chicken from the poaching liquid and discard the skins and bones. Cut the chicken flesh into strips, then set aside.

5 Melt the butter in a frying pan and fry the sliced leeks over a low heat, stirring occasionally, until soft.

6 Stir in the Cheddar, Parmesan and chopped parsley. Spread half the leek mixture over the cooked pastry base, leaving a border all the way round.

7 Cover the leek mixture with the chicken strips, then top with the remaining leek mixture. Mix together the wholegrain mustard, cornflour and double cream in a small bowl. Add seasoning to taste. Pour over the chicken and leek filling.

8 Moisten the edges of the cooked pastry base. Roll out the remaining pastry into a rectangle and use to cover the pie. Brush the lid of the pie with beaten egg and bake in the preheated oven for 30–40 minutes until the pie is golden and crisp. Serve hot, cut into generous square portions, with a mixed green side salad.

Curried Chicken and Apricot Pie

This pie is unusually sweet-sour and very more-ish. Use boneless turkey instead of chicken, if you wish.

INGREDIENTS

Serves 6

30ml/2 tbsp sunflower oil

1 large onion, chopped

450g/1lb chicken, boned and roughly chopped

15ml/1 tbsp curry paste or powder

30ml/2 tbsp apricot or peach chutney

115g/4oz/^{1}/2 cup ready-to-eat dried apricots, halved

115g/4oz cooked carrots, sliced

5ml/1 tsp mixed dried herbs

60ml/4 tbsp crème fraîche

350g/12oz ready-made shortcrust pastry

little egg or milk, to glaze

salt and black pepper

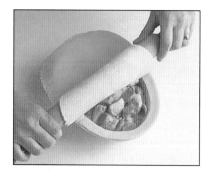

3 Roll out the pastry to 2.5cm/ 1in wider than the pie dish. Cut a strip of pastry from the edge. Damp the rim of the dish, press on the strip, then brush with water and place the sheet of pastry on top, press to seal.

4 Preheat the oven to 190°C/ 375°F/Gas 5. Trim off any excess pastry and use to make an attractive pattern on the top if you wish. Brush all over with beaten egg or milk and bake for 40 minutes, until crisp and golden.

1 Heat the oil in a large pan and fry the onion and chicken until just colouring. Add the curry paste or powder and fry for another 2 minutes.

2 Add the chutney, apricots, carrots, herbs and crème fraîche to the pan with seasoning. Mix well and then transfer to a deep 900ml–1.2 litre/1^1/2–2 pint/ 4–5 cup pie dish.

Hampshire Farmhouse Flan

*The lattice pastry topping makes
this flan look extra special.*

INGREDIENTS

Serves 4

225g/8oz/2 cups wholemeal flour

50g/2oz/^{1}/4 cup butter, cubed

50g/2oz/^{1}/3 cup lard

5ml/1 tsp caraway seeds

15ml/1 tbsp oil

1 onion, chopped

1 garlic clove, crushed

225g/8oz/2 cups chopped cooked
    chicken

75g/3oz/1^1/2 cups watercress leaves,
    chopped

grated rind of ^{1}/2 small lemon

2 eggs, lightly beaten

175ml/6fl oz/^{3}/4 cup double cream

45ml/3 tbsp natural yogurt

a good pinch of grated nutmeg

45ml/3 tbsp grated Caerphilly cheese

beaten egg, to glaze

salt and black pepper

3 Roll out the pastry and use to line an 18 x 28cm/7 x 11in loose-based flan tin. Reserve the trimmings. Prick the base and chill for 20 minutes. Place a baking sheet in the oven and preheat to 200°C/400°F/Gas 6.

4 Heat the oil in a frying pan and sauté the onions and garlic for 5–8 minutes, until just softened. Remove from the heat and cool.

5 Line the pastry case with greaseproof paper and fill with baking beans. Bake for 10 minutes, then remove the paper and beans and cook for 5 minutes.

6 Mix the onions, garlic, chicken, watercress and lemon rind. Spoon into the flan case. Beat the eggs, cream, yogurt, nutmeg, cheese and seasoning and pour over.

7 Roll out the pastry trimmings and cut out 1cm/^{1}/2in strips. Brush with egg, then lay in a lattice over the flan. Press the ends on to the pastry edge. Bake for 35 minutes, until the top is golden.

1 Place the flour in a bowl with a pinch of salt. Add the butter and lard and rub into the flour with your fingertips until the mixture resembles breadcrumbs. (Alternatively, you can use a blender or food processor for this.)

2 Stir in the caraway seeds and 45ml/3 tbsp iced water and mix to a firm dough. Knead lightly on a floured surface until smooth.

Chicken and Mushroom Pie

Use a mixture of dried and fresh mushrooms for this pie.

Serves 6

15g/^{1}/2oz/^{1}/4 cup dried porcini
   mushrooms
50g/2oz/^{1}/4 cup/4 tbsp butter
30ml/2 tbsp flour
250ml/8fl oz/1 cup chicken stock, warmed
50ml/2fl oz/^{1}/4 cup whipping cream or
   milk
1 onion, coarsely chopped
2 carrots, sliced
2 celery sticks, coarsely chopped
50g/2oz/^{3}/4 cup fresh mushrooms,
   quartered
450g/1lb/3 cups cooked chicken meat,
   cubed
50g/2oz/^{1}/2 cup shelled fresh or frozen
   peas
salt and black pepper
beaten egg, for glazing

For the crust
225g/8oz/2 cups flour
1.5ml/^{1}/4 tsp salt
115g/4oz/^{1}/2 cup cold butter, cut in pieces
50g/2oz/^{1}/3 cup lard
60–120ml/4–8 tbsp iced water

1 To make the crust, sift the flour and salt into a bowl. Cut in the butter and lard until the mixture resembles breadcrumbs. Sprinkle with 6 tbsp iced water and mix until the dough holds together. Add a little more water, if necessary, 1 tbsp at a time.

2 Gather the dough into a ball and flatten into a disk. Wrap in greaseproof paper and chill at least 30 minutes.

3 Place the porcini mushrooms in a small bowl. Add hot water to cover and soak until soft, about 30 minutes. Lift out of the water with a slotted spoon to leave any grit behind and drain. Discard the soaking water.

4 Preheat the oven to 190°C/ 375°F/Gas 5.

5 Melt 25g/1oz/2 tbsp of the butter in a heavy saucepan. Whisk in the flour and cook until bubbling, whisking constantly. Add the warm stock and cook over medium heat, whisking, until the mixture boils. Cook 2–3 minutes more. Whisk in the cream or milk. Season with salt and pepper. Put to one side.

6 Heat the remaining butter in a large non-stick frying pan until foamy. Add the onion and carrots and cook until softened, about 5 minutes. Add the celery and fresh mushrooms and cook 5 minutes more. Stir in the chicken, peas, and drained porcini mushrooms.

7 Add the chicken mixture to the sauce and stir. Taste for seasoning. Transfer to a rectangular 2.5 litre/4 pints/10 cup baking dish.

8 Roll out the dough to about 3mm/^{1}/8in thickness. Cut out a rectangle about 2.5cm/1in larger all around than the dish. Lay the rectangle of dough over the filling. Make a decorative crimped edge by pushing the index finger of one hand between the thumb and index finger of the other.

9 Cut several vents in the top crust to allow steam to escape. Brush with the egg to glaze.

10 Press together the dough trimmings, then roll out again. Cut into strips and lay them over the top crust. Glaze again. If desired, roll small balls of dough and set them in the "windows" in the lattice.

11 Bake until the top crust is browned, about 30 minutes. Serve the pie hot.

HOT
& SPICY

Cajun Chicken

Use cooked ham and prawns if you have them, but chicken and chorizo sausage are the main ingredients for this dish.

Serves 4

1.25kg/2¹/₂ lb fresh chicken

1¹/₂ onions

1 bay leaf

4 black peppercorns

1 parsley sprig

30ml/2 tbsp vegetable oil

2 garlic cloves, chopped

1 green pepper, seeded and chopped

1 celery stick, chopped

225g/8oz/1¹/₄ cups long grain rice

115g/4oz/1 cup chorizo sausage, sliced

115g/4oz/1 cup chopped, cooked ham

400g/14oz can chopped tomatoes with
   herbs

2.5ml/¹/₂ tsp hot chilli powder

2.5ml/¹/₂ tsp cumin seeds

2.5ml/¹/₂ tsp ground cumin

5ml/1 tsp dried thyme

115g/4oz/1 cup cooked, peeled prawns

dash of Tabasco sauce

chopped parsley, to garnish

1 Place the chicken in a large flameproof casserole and pour over 600ml/1 pint/2¹/₂ cups water. Add the half onion, the bay leaf, peppercorns and parsley and bring to the boil. Cover and simmer gently for about 1¹/₂ hours.

2 When the chicken is cooked lift it out of the stock, remove the skin and carcass and chop the meat. Strain the stock, leave to cool and reserve.

3 Chop the remaining onion and heat the oil in a large frying pan. Add the onion, garlic, green pepper and celery. Fry for about 5 minutes, then stir in the rice coating the grains with the oil. Add the sausage, ham and reserved chopped chicken and fry for a further 2–3 minutes, stirring frequently.

4 Pour in the tomatoes and 300ml/¹/₂ pint/1¹/₄ cups of the reserved stock and add the chilli, cumin and thyme. Bring to the boil, then cover and simmer gently for 20 minutes, or until the rice is tender and the liquid absorbed.

5 Stir in the prawns and Tabasco. Cook for a further 5 minutes, then season well and serve hot garnished with chopped parsley.

Spatchcocked Devilled Poussins

"Spatchcock", perhaps a corruption of the old Irish phrase "despatch a cock", refers to birds that are split and skewered flat for cooking.

Serves 4

15ml/1 tbsp English mustard powder
15ml/1 tbsp paprika
15ml/1 tbsp ground cumin
20ml/4 tsp tomato ketchup
15ml/1 tbsp lemon juice
65g/2¹/₂oz/5 tbsp butter, melted
4 poussins, about 450g/1lb each
salt

1 Mix together the mustard, paprika, cumin, ketchup, lemon juice and salt until smooth, then gradually stir in the butter.

2 Using game shears or strong kitchen scissors, split each poussin along one side of the backbone, then cut down the other side of the backbone to remove it.

3 Open out a poussin, skin side uppermost, then press down firmly with the heel of your hand. Pass a long skewer through one leg and out through the other to secure the bird open and flat. Repeat with the remaining birds.

4 Spread the mustard mixture evenly over the skin of the birds. Cover loosely and leave in a cool place for at least 2 hours. Preheat the grill.

5 Place the birds, skin side up, under the grill and cook for about 12 minutes. Turn over, baste and cook for a further 7 minutes, until the juices run clear.

COOK'S TIP

Spatchcocked poussins cook well on the barbecue. Make sure the coals are hot, then cook for 15–20 minutes, turning and basting frequently.

Moroccan Chicken Couscous

*A subtly spiced and fragrant dish
with a fruity sauce.*

INGREDIENTS

Serves 4

15ml/1 tbsp butter

15ml/1 tbsp sunflower oil

4 chicken portions, about 175g/6oz each

2 onions, finely chopped

2 garlic cloves, crushed

2.5ml/$^1/_2$ tsp ground cinnamon

1.5ml/$^1/_4$ tsp ground ginger

1.5ml/$^1/_4$ tsp ground turmeric

30ml/2 tbsp orange juice

10ml/2 tsp clear honey

salt

fresh mint sprigs, to garnish

For the couscous

350g/12oz/2 cups couscous

5ml/1 tsp salt

10ml/2 tsp caster sugar

30ml/2 tbsp sunflower oil

2.5ml/$^1/_2$ tsp ground cinnamon

pinch of grated nutmeg

15ml/1 tbsp orange flower water

30ml/2 tbsp sultanas

50g/2oz/$^1/_2$ cup chopped blanched
   almonds

45ml/3 tbsp chopped pistachios

1 Heat the butter and oil in a large pan and add the chicken portions, skin-side down. Fry for 3–4 minutes, until the skin is golden, then turn over.

2 Add the onions, garlic, spices and a pinch of salt and pour over the orange juice and 300ml/$^1/_2$ pint/1$^1/_4$ cups water. Cover and bring to the boil, then reduce the heat and simmer for about 30 minutes.

3 Meanwhile, place the couscous and salt in a bowl and cover with 350ml/12fl oz/1$^1/_2$ cups water. Stir once and leave to stand for 5 minutes. Add the caster sugar, 15ml/1 tbsp of the oil, the cinnamon, nutmeg, orange flower water and sultanas and mix well.

4 Heat the remaining 15ml/ 1 tbsp of the oil in a pan and lightly fry the almonds until golden. Stir into the couscous with the pistachios.

5 Line a steamer with grease-proof paper and spoon in the couscous. Sit the steamer over the chicken (or over a pan of boiling water) and steam for 10 minutes.

6 Remove the steamer and keep covered. Stir the honey into the chicken liquid and boil rapidly for 3–4 minutes. Spoon the couscous on to a warmed serving platter and top with the chicken, with a little of the sauce spooned over. Garnish with fresh mint and serve with the remaining sauce.

Spicy Masala Chicken

These chicken pieces are grilled and have a sweet-and-sour taste. They can be served cold with a salad and rice or hot with mashed potatoes.

Serves 6

12 chicken thighs
90ml/6 tbsp lemon juice
5ml/1 tsp chopped fresh root ginger
5ml/1 tsp chopped garlic
5ml/1 tsp crushed dried red chillies
5ml/1 tsp salt
5ml/1 tsp soft brown sugar
30ml/2 tbsp clear honey
30ml/2 tbsp chopped fresh coriander
1 green chilli, finely chopped
30ml/2 tbsp vegetable oil
fresh coriander sprigs, to garnish

1 Prick the chicken thighs with a fork, rinse, pat dry and set aside in a bowl.

2 In a large mixing bowl, make the marinade by mixing together the lemon juice, ginger, garlic, crushed dried red chillies, salt, sugar and honey.

3 Transfer the chicken thighs to the spice mixture and coat well. Set aside for about 45 minutes.

4 Preheat the grill to medium. Add the fresh coriander and chopped green chilli to the chicken thighs and place them in a flame-proof dish.

5 Pour any remaining marinade over the chicken and baste with the oil.

6 Grill the chicken thighs under the preheated grill for 15–20 minutes, turning and basting occasionally, until they are cooked through and browned.

7 Transfer the chicken to a serving dish and garnish with a few sprigs of fresh coriander.

Quick Chicken Curry

Curry powder can be bought in three different strengths – mild, medium and hot. Use the type you prefer to suit your taste.

INGREDIENTS

Serves 4
8 chicken legs (thighs and drumsticks)
30ml/2 tbsp vegetable oil
1 onion, thinly sliced
1 garlic clove, crushed
15ml/1 tbsp curry powder
15ml/1 tbsp plain flour
450ml/³/4 pint/1³/4 cups chicken stock
1 beefsteak tomato
15ml/1 tbsp mango chutney
15ml/1 tbsp lemon juice
salt and black pepper
plain boiled rice, to serve

1 Cut the chicken legs in half. Heat the oil in a large flame-proof casserole and brown the chicken pieces on all sides. Remove and keep warm.

2 Add the onion and crushed garlic to the casserole and cook until soft. Add the curry powder and cook gently for 2 minutes.

3 Add the flour, and gradually blend in the chicken stock and the seasoning.

4 Bring to the boil, replace the chicken pieces, cover and simmer for 20–30 minutes or until tender.

5 Skin the tomato by blanching in boiling water for 45 seconds, then run under cold water to loosen the skin. Peel and cut into small cubes.

6 Add to the chicken, with the mango chutney and lemon juice. Heat through gently and adjust the seasoning to taste. Serve with plenty of boiled rice and Indian pickles.

Tandoori Chicken Kebabs

This dish originates from the plains of the Punjab at the foot of the Himalayas. There food is tradition-ally cooked in clay ovens known as tandoors – hence the name.

INGREDIENTS

Serves 4

4 chicken breasts, about 175g/6oz each, boned and skinned

15ml/1 tbsp lemon juice

45ml/3 tbsp tandoori paste

45ml/3 tbsp natural yogurt

1 garlic clove, crushed

30ml/2 tbsp chopped fresh coriander

1 small onion, cut into wedges and separated into layers

a little oil, for brushing

salt and black pepper

fresh coriander sprigs, to garnish

pilau rice and naan bread, to serve

1 Chop the chicken breasts into 2.5cm/1in cubes, place in a bowl and add the lemon juice, tandoori paste, yogurt, garlic, coriander and seasoning. Cover and leave to marinate in the fridge for at least 2–3 hours.

2 Preheat the grill. Thread alternate pieces of chicken and onion on to four skewers.

3 Brush the onions with a little oil, lay the kebabs on a grill rack and cook under a high heat for about 10–12 minutes, turning once. Garnish the kebabs with fresh coriander and serve at once with pilau rice and naan bread.

Chinese Chicken with Cashew Nuts

A stir-fry of chicken with egg noodles, spring onions and cashews.

INGREDIENTS

Serves 4

4 chicken breasts about 175g/6oz each, boned, skinned and sliced into strips

3 garlic cloves, crushed

60ml/4 tbsp soy sauce

30ml/2 tbsp cornflour

225g/8oz/1 cup dried egg noodles

45ml/3 tbsp groundnut or sunflower oil

15ml/1 tbsp sesame oil

115g/4oz/1 cup roasted cashew nuts

6 spring onions, cut into 5cm/2in pieces and halved lengthways

spring onion curls and a little chopped red chilli, to garnish

1 Mix the chicken, garlic, soy sauce and cornflour in a bowl. Cover and chill for 30 minutes.

2 Bring a pan of water to the boil and add the noodles. Turn off the heat and leave to stand for 5 minutes. Drain well and reserve.

3 Heat the oils in a large frying pan and add the chicken and marinade. Stir-fry for about 3–4 minutes, or until golden brown.

4 Add the cashew nuts and spring onions to the pan or wok and stir-fry for 2–3 minutes.

5 Add the drained noodles and stir-fry for a further 2 minutes. Serve immediately, garnished with the spring onion curls and chopped red chilli.

Sweet and Sour Kebabs

This marinade contains sugar and will burn very easily, so grill the kebabs slowly, turning often. Serve with Harlequin Rice.

INGREDIENTS

Serves 4

2 chicken breasts, boned and skinned

8 pickling onions or 2 medium onions, peeled

4 rindless streaky bacon rashers

3 firm bananas

1 red pepper, seeded and sliced

For the marinade

30ml/2 tbsp soft brown sugar

15ml/1 tbsp Worcestershire sauce

30ml/2 tbsp lemon juice

salt and black pepper

For the Harlequin Rice

30ml/2 tbsp olive oil

225g/8oz/generous 1 cup cooked rice

115g/4oz/1 cup cooked peas

1 small red pepper, seeded and diced

1 Mix together the marinade ingredients. Cut each chicken breast into four pieces, add to the marinade, cover and leave for at least 4 hours or preferably overnight in the fridge.

2 Peel the pickling onions, blanch them in boiling water for 5 minutes and drain. If using medium onions, quarter them after blanching.

3 Cut each rasher of bacon in half. Peel the bananas and cut each into three pieces. Wrap a rasher of bacon around each piece of banana.

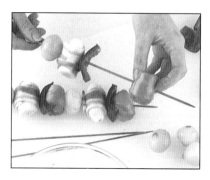

4 Thread on to metal skewers with the chicken pieces, onions and pepper slices. Brush with the marinade.

5 Grill or barbecue over low coals for 15 minutes, turning and basting frequently with the marinade. Keep warm while you prepare the rice.

6 Heat the oil in a frying pan and add the rice, peas and diced pepper. Stir until heated through and serve with the kebabs.

Chinese Chicken Wings

These are best eaten with fingers as a starter. Make sure you provide finger bowls and plenty of paper napkins, it could get messy.

Serves 4

12 chicken wings
3 garlic cloves, crushed
4cm/1 1/2in piece fresh root ginger, grated
juice of 1 large lemon
45ml/3 tbsp soy sauce
45ml/3 tbsp clear honey
2.5ml/1/2 tsp chilli powder
150ml/1/4 pint/2/3 cup chicken stock
salt and black pepper
lemon wedges, to garnish

3 Preheat the oven to 220°C/425°F/Gas 7. Remove the wings from the marinade and arrange in a single layer in a roasting tin. Bake for 20–25 minutes, basting at least twice with the marinade during cooking.

4 Place the wings on a serving plate. Add the stock to the marinade in the roasting tin, and bring to the boil. Cook to a syrupy consistency and spoon a little over the wings. Serve garnished with lemon wedges.

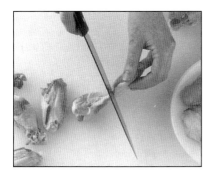

1 Remove the wing tips and use to make the stock. Cut the wings into two pieces.

2 Mix the remaining ingredients, apart from the stock, together and coat the chicken pieces in the mixture. Cover with clear film and marinate overnight.

Index